MEASURING CORPORATE DEFAULT RISK

Measuring Corporate Default Risk

DARRELL DUFFIE

OXFORD
UNIVERSITY PRESS

OXFORD

UNIVERSITY PRESS

Great Clarendon Street, Oxford OX2 6DP

Oxford University Press is a department of the University of Oxford.
It furthers the University's objective of excellence in research, scholarship,
and education by publishing worldwide in

Oxford New York

Auckland Cape Town Dar es Salaam Hong Kong Karachi
Kuala Lumpur Madrid Melbourne Mexico City Nairobi
New Delhi Shanghai Taipei Toronto

With offices in

Argentina Austria Brazil Chile Czech Republic France Greece
Guatemala Hungary Italy Japan Poland Portugal Singapore
South Korea Switzerland Thailand Turkey Ukraine Vietnam

Oxford is a registered trade mark of Oxford University Press
in the UK and in certain other countries

Published in the United States
by Oxford University Press Inc., New York

© Darrell Duffie 2011

British Library Cataloguing in Publication Data

Data available

Library of Congress Cataloging in Publication Data
Library of Congress Control Number: 2011929393

Typeset by SPI Publisher Services, Pondicherry, India
Printed in Great Britain
on acid-free paper by
CPI Antony Rowe, Chippenham, Wiltshire

ISBN 978-0-19-927923-4

1 3 5 7 9 10 8 6 4 2

To Malcolm

Contents

Acknowledgements

This monograph addresses the empirical estimation of corporate default risk. My audience is researchers from academia, regulatory authorities, and the financial services industry. A graduate-level background in probability theory is assumed for readers who plan to focus on the statistical methodology.

In addition to data obtained from common public sources, I rely heavily on corporate default event data from Moody's, to whom I am grateful. I am especially grateful to Richard Cantor and Roger Stein of Moody's, for their longstanding research support to myself and other members of the Moody's Academic Advisory Research Committee. In October 2008, I joined the board of directors of Moody's Corporation. Edward Altman generously provided additional helpful data on corporate default events. I am especially thankful for organizational and editorial guidance from Andrew Schuller, and for the hospitality of Andrew Schuller, Jenni Craig, and Colin Mayer while at Oxford University in June, 2004, when presenting the Clarendon Lectures in Finance, on which much of this manuscript is based. The research described here is the product of various collaborations with Sanjiv Das, Andreas Eckner, Guillaume Horel, Nikunj Kapadia, Leandro Saita, and Ke Wang, to whom I am extremely grateful. I am also thankful for excellent research assistance from Sergey Lobanov and Sabri Öncü, for helpful conversations on MCMC methods with Michael Johannes, Jun Liu, and Xiao-Li Meng, and for the opportunity to have collaborated on related default risk research projects with Antje Berndt, Rohan Douglas, Mark Ferguson, Nicolae Gârleanu, Ming Huang, David Lando, Lasse Heje Pedersen, Ken Singleton, and Costis Skiadas.

Darrell Duffie

Stanford
August, 2010

List of Figures

Figures 4.1, 5.1, 5.2, 5.3, 5.4 are taken from Das, Duffie, Kapadia, and Saita (2007).

Figures 4.2, 4.3, 7.7, A.1 are taken from Duffie, Saita, and Wang (2007).

Figures 7.1, 7.2, 7.3, 7.4, 7.5, 7.6, 7.8, 7.9, G.1, H.1, H.2, H.3 are taken from Duffie, Eckner, Horel, and Saita (2009).

List of Tables

Tables 4.1, 4.2, 7.1, F.1, G.1 are taken from Duffie, Eckner, Horel, and Saita (2009).
Tables 5.1, 5.2, 5.3, 5.4, B.1, C.1, C.2, C.3 are taken from Das, Duffie, Kapadia, and Saita
   (2007).

1

Objectives and Scope

Effective estimation of the likelihoods of default of individual corporate borrowers is crucial to those responsible for granting bank loans or investing in financial products exposed to corporate default. An ability to model the probability distribution of total default losses on portfolios of corporate loans, which depends on the measurement of default correlation across various firms, is an important input to the risk management of corporate loan portfolios, the determination of minimum capital requirements of financial institutions, and investment in structured credit products such as collateralized loan obligations that are exposed to multiple borrowers.

1.1 APPROACH

This book addresses the measurement of corporate default risk based on the empirical estimation of default intensity processes. The default intensity of a borrower is the mean rate of arrival of default, conditional on the available information. For example, a default intensity of 0.1 means an expected arrival rate of one default per 10 years, given all current information. Default intensities change with the arrival of new information about the borrower and its economic environment. I focus on methodologies for estimating default intensities and on some key empirical properties of corporate default risk. I pay special attention to the correlation of default risk across firms. The work summarized here was developed in a series of collaborations over roughly the past decade with Sanjiv Das, Andreas Eckner, Guillaume Horel, Nikunj Kapadia, Leandro Saita, and Ke Wang. Research on the measurement of corporate default risk remains active.

The data reveal, among other findings, that a substantial amount of power for predicting the default of a corporation can be obtained from the firm's "distance to default," a volatility-adjusted measure of leverage that is the basis of the theoretical models of corporate debt pricing of Black and Scholes (1973), Merton

(1974), Fisher, Heinkel, and Zechner (1989), and Leland (1994). Additional explanation is offered by a selection of macroeconomic variables and accounting ratios. Information relevant to the joint defaults of different firms that is not observable, or at least not captured by the chosen estimation approach, can be incorporated into a correlated default model through a statistical device known as "frailty." The last chapter shows that frailty contributes significantly to the likelihood of joint defaults of U.S. corporations.

An alternative approach is the estimation of a structural model of default, by which one directly captures how the managers of a firm opt for bankruptcy protection. For many practical purposes, structural empirical models of default have not yet matured sufficiently, given the complexity of most corporations and of the economic process of default, to be successfully applied to default risk estimation. Instead, the models explained here are based on reduced-form relationships between default risk and default predictors, particularly distance to default, that are suggested by structural models.

I suppose throughout that a firm's default intensity is of the form $\Lambda(X_t, \beta)$, where

- X_t is a list of firm-specific and macroeconomic default covariates, some of which are suggested by structural theories, in addition to unobservable covariates, and

- $\Lambda(\cdot, \beta)$ is a convenient *ad hoc* function, not necessarily based on a theory of the firm, depending on a parameter vector β to be estimated. Empirical results are also reported for a model estimated with non-parametric dependence of intensity on one of the key covariates, the distance to default.

Typical applications call for estimates of the likelihood of default (or joint default) over various time horizons. For this, it is also necessary to estimate the time-series behavior of the underlying covariate process X, which is treated here as a Markov process whose transition probabilities are governed by additional parameters to be estimated. With "frailty," default correlation is based on the assumption that some elements of the state vector X_t are not observable.

A structural approach could lead instead to an endogenously determined default intensity as a property of the decision problems faced by corporate managers, shareholders, creditors, and regulators. With this structural approach, the parameters to be estimated would specify the primitive technology of the firm, the contracting and capital-markets environment, and the preferences of the firm's managers and shareholders.

Structural model estimation offers the prospect of significant improvements in predictive power and should remain at the top of the research agenda for this subject area, despite not being the focus of the work presented here.

This book does not treat the estimation of the recovery of debt obligations in the event of default, a separate and important topic. Zhang (2009) provides an empirical model of corporate default recovery risk.

Statistical foundations are presented in a stand-alone series of chapters. A separate series of chapters contains the substantive empirical results. Neither of these two series of chapters needs to be read in order to obtain the thrust of the other.

1.2 STATISTICAL FOUNDATION CHAPTERS

Chapters 2, 3, and 6 provide a mathematical foundation for modeling and estimating default events with stochastic intensities. These chapters can be skipped by readers interested mainly in empirical content.

Chapter 2 provides the mathematical foundations for modeling the arrival of events with a stochastic intensity. The intensity of an event such as default is its conditional mean arrival rate λ_t, measured in events per year, given all information currently available to the observer. Under the doubly-stochastic assumption that we sometimes adopt, the probability of survival for t years is $E(e^{-\int_0^t \lambda(s)\,ds})$. Chapter 2 also presents the multi-firm version of the doubly-stochastic hypothesis, under which the sole source of default correlation between two firms is the dependence of their default intensities on common or correlated observable risk factors. The doubly-stochastic property rules out contagion as well as correlation induced by unobservable risk factors. This chapter includes an approach developed by Das, Duffie, Kapadia, and Saita (2007) for testing a model of the default intensity processes of a large number of borrowers.

Chapter 3 presents the theory underlying the maximum likelihood estimation of term structures of survival probabilities, including the dependence of default probability on time horizon. The methodology allows the events of concern to be censored by the disappearance of corporations from the data, due for instance to merger or acquisition. The idea is to estimate the parameter vector β determining the default intensity $\lambda_t = \Lambda(X_t, \beta)$ as well as the parameter vector γ determining the transition probabilities of the covariate process X, and then to use the maximum likelihood estimator of (β, γ) to estimate the survival probability $E(e^{-\int_0^t \lambda(s)\,ds})$, for a range of choices of the survival horizon t. The approach, from Duffie et al. (2007), allows the joint estimation of (β, γ) in a relatively tractable manner under the doubly-stochastic property by decomposing the problem into separate estimations of β and for γ.

Chapter 6 presents the foundations for frailty modeling of correlated default in a setting of stochastic intensities. The approach is to assume that default times are jointly doubly stochastic given extra information unavailable to the econometrician. This "hidden" information includes covariates that, although not directly observable, have conditional probability distributions that can be filtered from histories of default times and observable covariates. The dependence of default timing on unobservable covariates allows for sources of default correlation beyond those present in the observed covariates. The methodology relies on Markov Chain Monte Carlo (MCMC) techniques, provided in appendices, for evaluating likelihood functions and for filtering or smoothing hidden (frailty) state information.

1.3 SCOPE OF EMPIRICAL CHAPTERS

Chapters 4, 5, and 7 contain the substantive empirical results for North American non-financial corporations between 1979 and 2005.

Chapter 4 presents an estimated dynamic model of the term structures of conditional default probabilities. The results, based on Duffie, Saita, and Wang (2007) and Duffie, Eckner, Horel, and Saita (2009), show the significant dependence of default probabilities on a firm's distance to default (a volatility-adjusted leverage measure) and, to a lesser extent, on the firm's trailing stock return as well as various macroeconomic variables. In the structural models of Black and Scholes (1973), Merton (1974), Fisher, Heinkel, and Zechner (1989), and Leland (1994), the distance to default is a sufficient statistic for default probabilities. The estimated shape of the term structure of conditional default probabilities reflects the time-series behavior of the covariates, including the mean reversion of macroeconomic performance and leverage targeting by firms. The estimated term structures of default hazard rates are typically upward-sloping at business-cycle peaks and downward-sloping at business-cycle troughs, to a degree that depends on corporate leverage relative to its long-run target. Typical peak-to-trough variation in distances to default have a larger and more persistent impact on default probabilities than does business-cycle variation of the macro-covariates (after controlling for distance to default).

Chapter 5, based on Das, Duffie, Kapadia, and Saita (2007), provides a battery of tests of the ability of the model estimated in Chapter 4 to capture default correlation. Several of these tests are based on a time rescaling by which defaults arrive according to a constant-intensity Poisson process. Additional specification tests from Das, Duffie, Kapadia, and Saita (2007) are found in Appendix C.

The results of Chapter 5 show strong evidence of missing common or correlated default risk factors, some of which may not even have been contemporaneously available. Based on this idea, Chapter 7 provides estimates of a frailty-based model of joint default arrivals, in which default correlation can arise from variables that might have been available to the econometrician but were not included in the model, and also from additional unobservable sources of correlation. The results show substantial dependence of default intensities on common unobservable (or at least un-included) factors whose effects are condensed for modeling purposes into a single dynamic factor, parameterized as an Ornstein–Uhlenbeck frailty process. The estimated parameters governing the mean reversion and volatility of this frailty process, as well as the posterior (filtered) probability distribution of the frailty process, indicate substantial persistence and time variation in unobserved common sources of default risk. Appendices provide extensions of the model that allow for unobserved cross-sectional sources of variation in default intensity and non-linear dependence of a firm's default intensity on its distance to default.

Even after the financial crisis of 2007–2009, traders of structured credit products such as collateralized debt obligations (CDOs) that are directly exposed to default correlation have relied on copula models of default time correlation. As explained in Appendix B, a copula is a simple device for specifying the joint probability distribution of a collection of random variables with given marginal distributions. Despite its advantages for data structuring and for the rapid calculation of multi-firm default probabilities, the copula model is inherently unsuited to portfolio-based risk management and pricing applications, such as CDO pricing and value-at-risk measurement. A key shortcoming of the copula model is that it is unable, even in principle, to capture the risk of changes over time in conditional default probabilities. Models based on correlated intensity processes, although substantially more complicated to use than the industry-standard copula model, are now a sufficiently tractable alternative for many pricing and risk management applications. For example, Eckner (2009) shows how to model the pricing and risk management of CDOs with correlated default intensity processes.

1.4 HISTORICAL RESEARCH DEVELOPMENTS

Altman (1968) and Beaver (1968) were perhaps the first to estimate statistical models of the likelihoods of default of corporations, using financial accounting data. Lane et al. (1986) made an early contribution to the empirical literature on the probability distributions of corporate default times with their work on bank default prediction, using time-independent covariates. Lee and Urrutia (1996) introduced a duration model of default timing based on Weibull distributed default times. Duration models of default with time-varying covariates include those of McDonald and Van de Gucht (1999), who addressed the timing of high-yield bond defaults and call exercises. Duration models were used by

Shumway (2001), Kavvathas (2001), Chava and Jarrow (2004), and Hillegeist, Keating, Cram, and Lundstedt (2004) to predict bankruptcy. Shumway (2001) used a duration model with time-dependent covariates.

Each of these early studies took a "reduced-form" approach, modeling the dependence of default probabilities on explanatory variables through an econometric specification that does not directly model the incentives or ability of the borrower to pay its debt. Some structural models of default timing have the implication that a corporation defaults when its assets drop to a sufficiently low level relative to its liabilities. For example, the models of Black and Scholes (1973), Merton (1974), Fisher, Heinkel, and Zechner (1989), and Leland (1994) model the market value of a firm's assets as a geometric Brownian motion. In these models, a firm's conditional default probability is completely determined by its distance to default, which is the number of standard deviations of annual asset growth by which the asset level (or expected asset level at a given time horizon) exceeds an accounting-based measure of the firm's liabilities. An estimate of this default covariate, using market equity data and accounting data for liabilities, has been adopted in industry practice by Moody's in order to provide estimated probabilities of default for essentially all publicly traded firms. (See Crosbie and Bohn (2002) and Kealhofer (2003).)

In the context of the structural default model of Fisher, Heinkel, and Zechner (1989), Duffie and Lando (2001) modeled the conditional probability distribution of a default time for cases in which a firm's distance to default is imperfectly observed. This model implies the existence of a default intensity process that depends on the currently measured distance to default and on other covariates that may reveal additional information about the firm's condition. More generally, a firm's financial health may have multiple influences over time. For example, firm-specific, sector-wide, and macroeconomic state variables may all influence the evolution of corporate earnings and leverage.

The approach taken here, although not based directly on a structural model of default, is motivated by the structural approach through the inclusion of distance to default as a key covariate, and through the inclusion of additional observable and unobservable default covariates, in an attempt to capture sources of default risk that are not revealed by distance to default.

Duffie, Saita, and Wang (2007) introduced maximum likelihood estimation of term structures of default probabilities based on a joint model of stochastic default intensities and the dynamics of the underlying time-varying covariates. This work was based on the doubly-stochastic assumption, and therefore did not account for unobservable or missing covariates affecting default probabilities. With such incomplete observation, the arrival of a default leads, via Bayes' Rule, to a jump in the conditional distribution of hidden covariates, and therefore a jump in the conditional default probabilities of any other firms whose default intensities depend on the same unobservable covariates. For example, the collapses of Enron and WorldCom could have caused a sudden reduction in the perceived precision of accounting lever-age measures of other firms. Collin-Dufresne, Goldstein, and Helwege (2010) and Jorion and Zhang (2007) found that a major credit event at one firm is associated with significant increases in the credit spreads of other firms, consistent with the existence of a frailty effect for actual or risk-neutral default probabilities. Collin-Dufresne, Goldstein, and Huggonier (2004), Giesecke (2004), and Schönbucher (2003) explored learning-from-default interpreta-tions, based on the statistical modeling of frailty, under which default inten-sities include the expected effect of unobservable covariates. Yu (2005) found empirical evidence that, other things equal, a reduction in the measured precision of accounting variables is associated with a widening of credit spreads.

Delloy, Fermanian, and Sbai (2005) and Koopman, Lucas, and Monteiro (2008) introduced dynamic frailty models of default based on observations of credit ratings for each firm, and assuming that the intensities of changes from one rating to another depend on a common unobservable factor. Because credit ratings are incomplete and lagging indicators of credit quality, as shown for example by Lando and Skødeberg (2002), one would expect to find substan-tial frailty in ratings-based models such as these. Duffie, Eckner, Horel, and Saita (2009) extended the frailty-based approach to incorporate the variables used by Duffie, Saita, and Wang (2007), and still found substantial sources of frailty-based default correlation. Lando and Nielsen (2009) recently aug-mented the list of covariates used by Duffie, Eckner, Horel, and Saita (2009) with a selection of accounting ratios, and show an improvement in the ability of the model to capture default correlation with observable covariates. Koopman, Lucas, and Schwaab (2010) explored the role of frailty in the default experience of the recent financial crisis. Azizpour and Giesecke (2010) show the presence of frailty-based correlation in a version of the model that allows for the influ-ence of past default events. Although further improvements in model structure and covariate information are likely, it seems prudent when estimating the likelihood of large portfolio default losses to allow for unobserved sources of default correlation. The financial crisis of 2007–2009 was a severe lesson about potential sources of joint default risk that are not easily observed or captured with simple models.

2

Survival Modeling

This chapter presents probabilistic models of the arrival of events, such as defaults, that have a stochastic intensity. Readers interested mainly in empirical results could skip directly to Chapter 4.

2.1 STOCHASTIC INTENSITY

We fix a probability space $(\Omega, \mathcal{F}, P)$. The set Ω contains the possible states of the world. The set $\mathcal{F}$ consists of the subsets of Ω, called "events," to which a probability can be assigned. The probability measure $P : \mathcal{F} \to \mathbb{R}$ assigns a probability $P(A)$ to each event A. We also fix an information filtration $\{\mathcal{G}_t : t \geq 0\}$, satisfying the usual conditions,[1] that specifies for each time t the set $\mathcal{G}_t$ of events that are observable at that time.

Given a stopping time τ, for instance a default time, we say that a progressively measurable[2] non-negative process λ is the *intensity* of τ if a martingale M is defined by

$$M_t = 1_{\{\tau \leq t\}} - \int_0^t \lambda_s 1_{\{\tau > s\}} \, ds, \qquad (2.1)$$

where, for any event A, the indicator 1_A has an outcome of 1 on the event A and zero otherwise. This means that at any time t before τ, conditional on the current information $\mathcal{G}_t$, the mean rate of arrival of default is λ_t. For example, with time measured in years, an intensity of $\lambda_t = 0.1$ means that default arrives at a conditional mean rate of once every 10 years, given all information available at time t. This interpretation of the intensity is justified as follows. Consider

---

[1] The "usual conditions" are given by Protter (2004).
[2] A process $\lambda : \Omega \times [0, \infty) \to \mathbb{R}$ is said to be progressively measurable if it is a jointly measurable function and if, for each time t, the random variable $\lambda(t) = \lambda_t = \lambda(\cdot, t) : \Omega \to \mathbb{R}$ is $\mathcal{G}_t$-measurable, which means that λ_t depends only on the information available at time t.

some time horizons t and $u > t$. The martingale property for M means that $E(M_u - M_t \mid \mathcal{G}_t) = 0$, which implies that

$$E(1_{\{t < \tau \le u\}} \mid \mathcal{G}_t) = E\left(\int_t^u \lambda_s 1_{\{\tau > s\}} \, ds \;\middle|\; \mathcal{G}_t\right).$$

On the event $\{\tau > t\}$, the conditional mean rate of arrival of default at time t is therefore (almost everywhere)

$$\frac{d}{du} E(1_{\{t < \tau \le u\}} \mid \mathcal{G}_t)\Big|_{u = t+} = \lambda_t. \tag{2.2}$$

Similarly, because the conditional probability of default within Δ years is

$$P(\tau \in (t, t + \Delta] \mid \mathcal{G}_t) = E(1_{\{t < \tau \le t + \Delta\}} \mid \mathcal{G}_t),$$

we see from (2.2) that, on the event that default occurs after the conditioning time t, the default intensity λ_t is the rate of change of the increase in the conditional default probability as the time horizon Δ increases from 0. If λ has a continuous sample path, this further implies the approximation $\lambda_t \Delta$ for the conditional probability of default within a time period of small duration Δ.

A default intensity that is constant over time implies a Poisson model of default arrival in which the time until default is exponentially distributed with a mean equal to the reciprocal of the intensity. Realistically, however, default intensity processes change randomly over time with the arrival of new information about the prospects of the borrowers. For a public corporation, this new information includes the financial accounting reports of the firm, the stock price of the firm, macroeconomic performance indicators, and other news announcements relevant to the performance of the firm or its industry.

Because default intensities measure only the immediate expected arrival rate of default, some method is needed to link the behavior of default intensity processes to probabilities of default over distinct time horizons, such as the time to maturity of a bond. This is the subject of the next section.

2.2 DOUBLY-STOCHASTIC EVENT TIMING

In applications, we often consider the special case of an intensity process of the form $\lambda_t = f(X_t)$, where X is a Markov process in some state space D and where $f : D \to [0, \infty)$. For example, if τ is the default time of a firm, the covariate vector X_t would typically include a list of firm-specific and macroeconomic variables that help forecast that firm's default.

We say that a stopping time τ with intensity λ is *doubly-stochastic, driven by X*, if, conditional on the covariate path $X = \{X_t : t \geq 0\}$, τ is the first event time of some Poisson process with time-varying[3] intensity $\{\lambda_t : t \geq 0\}$. This Poisson property implies that

$$P(\tau > t \mid X) = e^{-\int_0^t \lambda(s)\,ds}. \tag{2.3}$$

Applying the law of iterated expectations,

$$P(\tau > t) = E[P(\tau > t \mid X)] = E\left(e^{-\int_0^t \lambda(s)\,ds}\right). \tag{2.4}$$

Similarly, on the event $\{\tau > t\}$,

$$P(\tau > u \mid \mathcal{G}_t) = E\left(e^{-\int_t^u \lambda(s)\,ds} \;\Big|\; \mathcal{G}_t\right) = E\left(e^{-\int_t^u \lambda(s)\,ds} \;\Big|\; X_t\right). \tag{2.5}$$

The doubly-stochastic property offers substantial tractability. For the case $\lambda_t = f(X_t)$, the survival probability can be computed from (2.5) using the backward Kolmogorov equation associated with X. For special cases in which $\lambda_t = a + b \cdot X_t$ and where X_t is an affine process, the survival probability (2.5) can be computed explicitly in the form $e^{\alpha(t,u)+\beta(t,u)\cdot X(t)}$, for deterministic coefficients $\alpha(t,u)$ and $\beta(t,u)$ that can be easily calculated. Examples are given by Duffie, Pan, and Singleton (2000).

Stopping times $\tau_1, \ldots, \tau_n$ that are doubly stochastic driven by X with respective intensities $\lambda_1, \ldots, \lambda_n$ are said to be *jointly* doubly stochastic if these times are X-conditionally independent. An implication is that $\tau_1, \ldots, \tau_n$ are correlated only through the joint dependence of their intensities on the covariate process X. For example, for any time t,

$$P(\tau_i > t, \tau_j > t) = E[P(\tau_i > t, \tau_j > t \mid X)]$$
$$= E\left(e^{-\int_0^t \lambda_i(s)\,ds} e^{-\int_0^t \lambda_j(s)\,ds}\right)$$
$$= E\left(e^{-\int_0^t [\lambda_i(s)+\lambda_j(s)]\,ds}\right).$$

Likewise, on the event $\{\tau_i > t, \tau_j > t\}$,

$$P(\tau_i > u, \tau_j > u \mid \mathcal{G}_t) = E\left(e^{-\int_t^u [\lambda_i(s)+\lambda_j(s)]\,ds} \;\Big|\; \mathcal{G}_t\right).$$

Again, this calculation is quite tractable in some specific Markov settings.

---

[3] A counting process K is Poisson if its intensity process c is deterministic, if its increments over disjoint time intervals are independent, and if, whenever $t > s$, $K_t - K_s$ is distributed as a Poisson random variable with parameter $\int_s^t c(u)\,du$. A random variable J has the Poisson distribution with parameter γ if, for any integer k, we have $P(J = k) = e^{-\gamma k}/k$

2.3 CENSORING

In statistical applications, observations can be censored, meaning removed from the relevant sample, possibly at random times. For example, a firm might disappear from the sample when merged or acquired, before it might have otherwise defaulted.

Suppose that a given firm with default time τ is censored at some stopping time T. The firm thus exits from the sample at $\min(\tau, T)$. We suppose for modeling simplicity that the default time τ and censoring time T are jointly doubly stochastic, driven by some Markov process X, with respective intensities λ and α.

We will later estimate empirical models in which $X_t = (U_t, Y_t)$, where U_t is firm-specific and Y_t is macroeconomic, and will consider an econometrician equipped with the censored information filtration $\{\mathcal{F}_t : t \geq 0\}$, taking $\mathcal{F}_t$ to be generated by the macro-variables $\{Y_s : s \leq t\}$ and the firm-specific observations

$$\{(U_s, 1_{\{\tau \geq s\}}, 1_{\{T \geq s\}}) \; : \; s \leq \min(t, \tau, T)\}.$$

On the event $\{\tau > t, T > t\}$ of survival to t, we will now show that the conditional probability of the event $\{\tau > u, T > u\}$ of survival to a future time u is

$$p(X_t, t, u) = E\left(e^{-\int_t^u [\lambda(s) + \alpha(s)]\, ds} \; \middle| \; \mathcal{G}_t\right), \tag{2.6}$$

using the independence of τ and T given X, and similarly that the conditional probability of default by time u is

$$q(X_t, t, u) = E\left(\int_t^u e^{-\int_t^v [\lambda(s) + \alpha(s)]\, ds} \lambda_v \, dv \; \middle| \; \mathcal{G}_t\right), \tag{2.7}$$

bearing in mind that the default cannot occur if the firm first exits at the censoring time T.

Proposition 1. *On the event* $\{\tau > t, T > t\}$ *of survival to t, the censored conditional joint survival probability is*

$$P(\tau > u, T > u \,|\, \mathcal{F}_t) = p(X_t, t, u),$$

where $p(X_t, t, u)$ *is given by (2.6), and the censored conditional default probability is*

$$P(\tau < u \,|\, \mathcal{F}_t) = q(X_t, t, u),$$

where $q(X_t, t, u)$ *is given by (2.7).*

Proof: We begin by verifying (2.6) and (2.7), that is, conditioning instead on the uncensored information set $\mathcal{G}_t$, and later show that the same calculation applies with censored conditioning.

The first calculation (2.6) is from the fact that τ and T are jointly doubly stochastic. For the second calculation (2.7), let $M = 1_{\{T \leq t\}}$ and $N = 1_{\{\tau \leq t\}}$. We use the fact that, conditional on the path of X, the (improper) density evaluated at any time $z > t$ of the default time τ, using the X-conditional independence of M and N is, with the standard abuse of notation,

$$P(\tau \in dz \mid X, \tau > t, T > t) = P(\inf\{u : N_u \neq N_t\} \in dz, M_z = M_t \mid X)$$

$$= P(\inf\{u : N_u \neq N_t\} \in dz \mid X) P(M_z = M_t \mid X)$$

$$= e^{-\int_t^z \lambda(u)\, du} \lambda(z)\, dz\; e^{-\int_t^z \alpha(u)\, du}$$

$$= e^{-\int_t^z [\alpha(u) + \lambda(u)]\, du} \lambda_z\, dz.$$

From the doubly-stochastic property, conditioning also on $\mathcal{G}_t$ has no effect on this calculation, so, on the event $\{\min(\tau, T) > t\}$,

$$P(\tau \in [t, u] \mid \mathcal{G}_t, X) = \int_t^u e^{-\int_t^z [\alpha(u) + \lambda(u)]\, du} \lambda_z\, dz. \qquad (2.8)$$

Now, taking the expectation of this conditional probability given $\mathcal{G}_t$ only, using the law of iterated expectations, leaves $q(X_t, t, u)$.

On the event $\{\tau > t, T > t\}$, the conditioning information in $\mathcal{F}_t$ and $\mathcal{G}_t$ coincides. That is, every event contained by $\{\tau > t, T > t\}$ that is in $\mathcal{G}_t$ is also in $\mathcal{F}_t$. The result follows. $\qquad \square$

2.4 HAZARD RATE

The *hazard rate* at some future date s of a random time τ that has a probability density function $f(\cdot)$ is the mean rate of arrival of τ conditional on survival to s. Using Bayes' Rule, this hazard rate is

$$H(s) = \frac{1}{du} P(\tau \in (s, s + du] \mid \tau > s) = \frac{f(s)}{\int_s^\infty f(t)\, dt}.$$

The hazard rate $H(s)$ is equivalent to the intensity of τ at time s that is associated with the artificially restricted information filtration $\{\mathcal{H}_t : t \geq 0\}$ that would apply if one's only source of information is the arrival of default. That is, $\mathcal{H}_t$ is the set of events generated by $\{1_{\{\tau < s\}} : 0 \leq s \leq t\}$.

In the setting of Proposition 1, the s-year hazard rate $h(X_t, t, s)$ of default, conditioning on the censored information available at time t, is defined on the event $\{\tau > t, T > t\}$ by

$$
\begin{aligned}
h(X_t, t, s) &= \frac{1}{du} P(\tau \in (t+s, t+s+du] \mid \mathcal{F}_t, \tau > t+s, T > t+s) \\
&= \frac{q_u(X_t, t, t+s)}{p(X_t, t, t+s)} \\
&= \frac{E(e^{-\int_t^{t+s}[\lambda(u)+\alpha(u)]\,du}\, \lambda_{t+s} \mid X_t)}{E(e^{-\int_t^{t+s}[\lambda(u)+\alpha(u)]\,du} \mid X_t)}.
\end{aligned}
$$

Although this calculation is explicit in common affine intensity models, it will be implemented numerically in Chapter 7 for a specification in which default intensities have a log-normal probability distribution, or have a numerically filtered conditional probability distribution that is based on an unconditional distribution that is log-normal.

2.5 TIME RESCALING FOR POISSON DEFAULTS

We finish the chapter with a result that will serve as the basis of a joint specification test of measured default intensities.

We suppose that $\tau_1, \ldots, \tau_n$ are the default times of n borrowers, with respective intensities $\lambda_1, \ldots, \lambda_n$. We consider a change of time scale under which the passage of one unit of "new time" coincides with a period of calendar time over which the total of all surviving firms' default intensities accumulates by one unit. Provided that $P(\tau_i = \tau_j) = 0$ whenever $i \neq j$, the arrivals of defaults constitute a standard (constant mean arrival rate) Poisson process if time is rescaled in this manner. For example, fixing any scalar $c > 0$, we can define successive non-overlapping time intervals each lasting for c units of new time (corresponding to calendar time intervals that each include an accumulated total default intensity, across all surviving firms, of c), this time change implies that the number of defaults in the successive time intervals (N_1 defaults in the first interval lasting for c units, N_2 defaults in the second interval, and so on) are independent Poisson distributed random variables with mean c.

In Chapter 5, we use this time change property as the basis for tests of whether the default intensities we estimate for North American public corporations are missing the effect of some correlating information. Das, Duffie, Kapadia, and Saita (2007) first applied this specification test under the assumption that default times are doubly stochastic. Lando and Nielsen (2009) noted that the same time change applies under the much weaker assumption that $P(\tau_i = \tau_j) = 0$ whenever $i \neq j$, as a consequence of a result of Meyer (1971).

Proposition 2. *Suppose that $\tau_1, \ldots, \tau_n$ are default times with respective strictly positive intensities $\lambda_1, \ldots, \lambda_n$. Suppose that $P(\tau_i = \tau_j) = 0$ for $i \neq j$. Let $K(t) = \#\{i : \tau_i \leq t\}$ be the cumulative number of defaults by t, and let $U(t) = \int_0^t \sum_{i=1}^n \lambda_i(u) 1_{\tau_i > u} \, du$ be the cumulative aggregate intensity of surviving firms, to time t. Then $J = \{J(s) = K(U^{-1}(s)) : s \geq 0\}$ is a Poisson process with rate parameter 1.*

Exercises

1.1 Fixing a probability space and information filtration, suppose that $\tau_1, \ldots, \tau_n$ have respective intensities $\lambda_1, \ldots, \lambda_n$, and that $P(\tau_i = \tau_j) = 0$ for $i \neq j$. Show that $\min(\tau_1, \ldots, \tau_n)$ has intensity $\lambda_1 + \cdots + \lambda_n$.

1.2 In the setting of Exercise 1.1, show that the condition $P(\tau_i = \tau_j) = 0$ applies if the stopping times are jointly doubly stochastic.

1.3 Consider a random time τ with a probability density function f. Fix the information filtration $\{\mathcal{H}_t : t \geq 0\}$ that is defined by letting $\mathcal{H}_t$ be the σ-algebra generated by the history $\{1_{\{\tau < s\}} : 0 \leq s \leq t\}$ of survival events. Let

$$H(t) = \frac{f(t)}{\int_t^\infty f(u) \, du}.$$

By constructing an appropriate martingale, use the definition of an intensity process to show that the deterministic process H is the intensity of τ.

3

How to Estimate Default Intensity Processes

We turn to the problem of statistical estimation. Our main objective in this chapter is to outline the methodology developed by Duffie, Saita, and Wang (2007) for the maximum likelihood estimation of term structures of conditional default probabilities. This calls not only for the estimation of default intensities at each point in time, but also depends on estimation of the probabilistic behavior of default intensities over time. Assuming a doubly-stochastic model, we show how to decompose the estimation problem into two separate econometric problems: (i) estimate the parameter vector β determining the dependence of each default intensity $\Lambda(X_t, \beta)$ on the underlying Markov state vector X_t, and (ii) estimate the probabilistic time-series behavior of X_t.

The methodology outlined here may be useful in other subject areas requiring estimators of multi-period survival probabilities based on intensities that depend on covariates with pronounced time-series dynamics. Examples might include labor mobility and health studies.

3.1 THE MAXIMUM LIKELIHOOD APPROACH

We fix some probability space $(\Omega, \mathcal{F}, P)$ and information filtration $\{\mathcal{G}_t : t \geq 0\}$. For a given stopping time τ, say a default time, we wish to estimate the term structure $\{P(\tau > t) : t \geq 0\}$ of survival probabilities. We suppose that τ is doubly stochastic driven by a d-dimensional Markov process X with intensity $\Lambda(X_t; \beta)$, where $\beta \in \mathbb{R}^\ell$ is a vector of parameters. We suppose for simplicity that X is constant between integer observation times $1, 2, \ldots$

Despite certain advantages offered by a Bayesian statistical approach, we adopt a simpler frequentist statistical approach, as follows. The "true" probability measure P is not known, but rather is one of a family $\{P_\theta : \theta \in \Theta\}$ of probability measures, depending on a parameter vector of the form

$$\theta = (\beta, \gamma) \in B \times \Gamma \subset \mathbb{R}^\ell \times \mathbb{R}^m.$$

The parameter vector $\theta = (\beta, \gamma)$ determines the probability distribution of τ through two channels:

1. Dependence of the default intensity $\lambda_t = \Lambda(X_t; \beta)$ on $\beta \in B \subset \mathbb{R}^\ell$, where $\Lambda : \mathbb{R}^d \times B \to [0, \infty)$.

2. Dependence on the second parameter component γ of the conditional probability density function $\phi(X_k, \cdot; \gamma)$ of X_{k+1} given X_k, where $\phi : \mathbb{R}^d \times \mathbb{R}^d \times \Gamma \to [0, \infty)$.

Our objective is to first estimate the "true" parameter vector θ^*, and then, based on this parameter estimate, obtain estimates of default probabilities over various time horizons, among other properties of the true probability measure $P = P_{\theta^*}$.

In addition to observations of the covariates $X_1, X_2, \ldots, X_k$, for k time periods, one's data include observations, possibly censored, of default times $\tau_1, \ldots, \tau_n$ whose intensities depend on X in the same manner as the stopping time τ of concern. Duffie, Saita, and Wang (2007) showed that a key advantage of the doubly-stochastic property is the ability to reduce the potentially complex joint maximum likelihood estimation of (β, γ) into simpler separate maximum likelihood estimations of β and γ, as follows.

Ignoring censoring for now, the likelihood to be maximized by choice of the parameter vector (β, γ) is the joint probability density of $(X, \tau_1, \ldots, \tau_n)$ under the probability measure $P_{(\beta, \gamma)}$, which is denoted $\mathcal{L}(X, \tau_1, \ldots, \tau_n; \beta, \gamma)$. Using Bayes Rule and the doubly-stochastic property,

$$\mathcal{L}(X, \tau_1, \ldots, \tau_n; \beta, \gamma) = \mathcal{L}(\tau_1, \ldots, \tau_n \mid X; \beta) \times \mathcal{L}(X; \gamma), \qquad (3.1)$$

indicating notationally that the conditional likelihood of $\tau_1, \ldots, \tau_n$ given X does not depend on γ and that the likelihood of X does not depend on β. Because the log likelihood

$$\log \mathcal{L}(X, \tau_1, \ldots, \tau_n; \beta, \gamma) = \log \mathcal{L}(\tau_1, \ldots, \tau_n \mid X; \beta) + \log \mathcal{L}(X; \gamma) \qquad (3.2)$$

has a first term that does not involve γ and a second does not involve β, the total log likelihood (3.2) is maximized by solving the respective traditional statistical problems

$$\sup_{\beta} \; \log \mathcal{L}(\tau_1, \ldots, \tau_n \mid X; \beta) \qquad (3.3)$$

and

$$\sup_{\gamma} \; \log \mathcal{L}(X; \gamma). \qquad (3.4)$$

Problem (3.3) is a relatively standard duration model with time-varying covariates, as treated for instance in Andersen, Borgan, Gill, and Keiding (1992).

The remaining econometric problem (3.4) can be reduced to a time-series problem that is as tractable as allowed by one's model of the covariate state process X.

For example, suppose the stopping times $\tau_1, \ldots, \tau_n$ have respective intensities $\Lambda_1(X_t, \beta), \ldots, \Lambda_n(X_t, \beta)$. In the simplest case of no censoring, Proposition 1 and the conditional independence of $\tau_1, \ldots, \tau_n$ given X imply that

$$\mathcal{L}(\tau_1, \ldots, \tau_n \mid \tilde{X}; \theta) = \prod_{i=1}^{n} e^{-\int_0^{\tau_i} \Lambda_i(X(t); \beta) \, dt} \Lambda_i(X(\tau_i); \beta). \qquad (3.5)$$

The Markov property of X implies that

$$\mathcal{L}(X; \gamma) = \prod_{j=1}^{k} \phi(X_{j-1}, X_j; \gamma). \qquad (3.6)$$

Maximizing the likelihoods (3.5) and (3.6) corresponds to standard statistical problems to which traditional methods can be applied. Under technical conditions, maximum likelihood estimation is efficient.

3.2 DATA STRUCTURE AND CENSORING

We now allow for censorship of information relevant to the default τ_i of the i-th firm at some stopping time S_i, which could be when the firm is merged, acquired, or otherwise disappears from the data. Under the true probability measure generating the data, the event times $S_1, \tau_1, S_2, \tau_2, \ldots, S_n, \tau_n$ are assumed to be doubly stochastic driven by X, with respective intensities $\alpha_1, \lambda_1, \ldots, \alpha_n, \lambda_n$.

As for the composition of the covariate process X, we suppose that

$$X_t = (U_{1t}, \ldots, U_{nt}, Y_t),$$

where Y_t is a "macro-covariate," observable for all t, and where U_{it} is a vector of covariates specific to firm i, such as leverage, volatility, cash-flow, expenses, management quality, sector identity, and so on. Naturally, U_{it} is censored at $\min(S_i, \tau_i)$.

For each firm i, we let $Z_{it} = (U_{it}, Y_t)$, and for simplicity assume that $\{Z_{i1}, Z_{i2}, Z_{i3}, \ldots\}$ is a discrete-time Markov process valued in $\mathbb{R}^{d(i)}$, for some integer $d(i)$. We assume, moreover, that $\lambda_{it} = \Lambda_i(Z_{i,k(t)}, \beta)$ and that $\alpha_{it} = A_i(Z_{i,k(t)}, \beta)$, where $k(t)$ is the largest integer less than t, for some

$$\Lambda_i : \mathbb{R}^{d(i)} \times B \to [0, \infty), \qquad A_i : \mathbb{R}^{d(i)} \times B \to [0, \infty).$$

This allows for firms that differ with respect to the parametric dependence of intensities on covariates and also with regard to the probability transition distributions of the Markov covariate processes Z_i. For example, one type of firm may have a default intensity that is more sensitive to leverage than another, and different types of firms may target different leverage ratios. In the end, however, for identification and consistency, one must assume that the number of types of firms is small relative to the total number of firms.

The econometrician's information set $\mathcal{F}_t$ at time t is that generated by

$$\mathcal{I}_t = \{Y_s : s \leq t\} \cup \mathcal{J}_{1t} \cup \mathcal{J}_{2t} \cup \cdots \cup \mathcal{J}_{nt},$$

where the information set for firm i is

$$\mathcal{J}_{it} = \{(1_{\{S_i < s\}}, 1_{\{\tau_i < s\}}, U_{is}) : t_i \leq s \leq \min(S_i, \tau_i, t)\},$$

and where t_i is the time of first appearance of firm i in the data set. For simplicity, we take t_i to be deterministic, but our results would extend to treat left censoring of each firm at a stopping time, under suitable conditional independence assumptions.

In order to simplify the estimation of the time-series model for covariates, we suppose that the macro-covariate process $\{Y_1, Y_2, \ldots\}$ is itself a time-homogeneous (discrete-time) Markov process.

Conditional on the list $Z_k = (Z_{1k}, \ldots, Z_{nk})$ of all firms' state variables available at time k, we suppose that Z_{k+1} has a joint density $f(\cdot \mid Z_k; \gamma)$, for some parameter vector γ to be estimated. This allows for conditional correlation between $U_{i,k+1}$ and $U_{j,k+1}$ given (Y_k, U_{ik}, U_{jk}).

3.3 CALCULATION OF THE LIKELIHOOD

As a notational convenience, whenever $K \subset L \subset \{1, \ldots, n\}$ we let

$$f_{KL}(\cdot \mid Y_k, \{U_{ik} : i \in L\}; \gamma)$$

denote the joint density of $(Y_{k+1}, \{U_{i,k+1} : i \in K\})$ given Y_k and $\{U_{ik} : i \in L\}$, which is a property of (in effect, a marginal of) $f(\cdot \mid Z_k; \gamma)$. In our application to North American default data in Chapter 4, we will further assume that $f(\cdot \mid z; \gamma)$ is a joint-normal density, which makes the marginal density function $f_{KL}(\cdot \mid y, \{u_i : i \in L\})$ an easily-calculated joint normal.

For additional convenient notation, let $R(k) = \{i : \min(\tau_i, S_i) > k\}$ denote the set of firms that survive to at least period k. We further let $\tilde{U}_k = \{U_{ik} : i \in R(k)\}$, $S_i(t) = \min(t, S_i)$, $S(t) = (S_1(t), \ldots, S_n(t))$, and likewise define $\tau_i(t)$ and $\tau(t)$. Under our doubly-stochastic assumption, the likelihood for the information set $\mathcal{I}_t$ is

$$\mathcal{L}(\mathcal{I}_t; \gamma, \beta) = \mathcal{L}(\tilde{U}, Y; \gamma) \times \mathcal{L}(S(t), \tau(t) \mid (Y, \tilde{U}); \beta), \qquad (3.7)$$

where

$$\mathcal{L}(\tilde{U}, Y; \gamma) = \prod_{k=0}^{k(t)} f_{R(k+1),R(k)}(Y_{k+1}, \tilde{U}_{k+1} \mid Y_k, \tilde{U}_k; \gamma) \qquad (3.8)$$

and

$$\mathcal{L}(S(t), \tau(t) \mid (Y, \tilde{U}); \beta) = \prod_{i=1}^{n} G_{it}(\beta), \qquad (3.9)$$

for

$$G_{it}(\beta) = \exp\left(-\int_{t_i}^{T_i} (A_i(Z_{i,k(s)}; \beta) + \Lambda_i(Z_{i,k(s)}; \beta))\, ds\right)$$

$$\times \left(1_{\{T_i = t\}} + A_i(Z_{i,S_i}; \beta)1_{\{T_i = S_i\}} + \Lambda_i(Z_{i,\tau_i}; \beta)1_{\{T_i = \tau_i\}}\right),$$

where $T_i = \min(S_i, \tau_i, t)$ is the last sample date for firm i.

Because of this structure for the likelihood, we can decompose the overall maximum likelihood estimation problem into the separate problems

$$\sup_{\gamma} \mathcal{L}(\tilde{U}, Y; \gamma) \qquad (3.10)$$

and

$$\sup_{\beta} \mathcal{L}(S(t), \tau(t) \mid (Y, \tilde{U}); \beta). \qquad (3.11)$$

Further simplification is obtained by taking the parameter vector β determining intensity dependence on covariates to be of the decoupled form $\beta = (\mu, \nu)$, with

$$\alpha_{it} = A_i(X_{it}; \mu); \qquad \lambda_{it} = \Lambda_i(X_{it}; \nu). \qquad (3.12)$$

(This involves a slight abuse of notation.) This means that the choice of parameter vector ν determining the intensity of τ_i does not restrict the selection of the parameter vector μ determining the intensity of S_i, and *vice versa*. An examination of the structure of (3.11) reveals that this decoupling assumption allows problem (3.11) to be further decomposed into the pair of problems

$$\sup_{\mu} \prod_{i=1}^{n} e^{-\int_{t_i}^{T_i} A_i(X_i(u); \mu)\, du} \left(1_{\{T_i < S_i\}} + A_i(X_i(S_i); \mu)1_{\{T_i = S_i\}}\right) \qquad (3.13)$$

and

$$\sup_{\nu} \prod_{i=1}^{n} e^{-\int_{t_i}^{T_i} \Lambda_i(X_i(u);\nu) \, du} \left(1_{\{T_i < \tau_i\}} + \Lambda_i(X_i(\tau_i); \nu)1_{\{T_i = \tau_i\}}\right). \qquad (3.14)$$

We have the following result, which summarizes our parameter-fitting algorithm.

Proposition 3. *Solutions γ^* and β^* of the respective maximum likelihood problems (3.10) and (3.11) collectively form a solution to the overall maximum likelihood problem*

$$\sup_{\gamma,\beta} \mathcal{L}(\mathcal{I}_t; \gamma, \beta). \qquad (3.15)$$

Under the parameter-decoupling assumption (3.12), solutions μ^* and ν^* to the maximum likelihood problems (3.13) and (3.14), respectively, form a solution $\beta^* = (\mu^*, \nu^*)$ to problem (3.11).

Each of these optimization problems is solved numerically. The decomposition of the MLE optimization problem given by Proposition 3 allows the individual numerical searches for γ^*, μ^*, and ν^* to be done in relatively low-dimensional parameter spaces.

3.4 TERM STRUCTURES OF DEFAULT PROBABILITIES

Given a maximum likelihood estimator θ^* for a parameter θ, the maximum likelihood estimator of $g(\theta)$, for some smooth function $g(\cdot)$, is $g(\theta^*)$. Thus, in the setting of Proposition 1 (Chapter 2) and under our statistical assumptions, given the maximum likelihood estimator $\theta = (\gamma, (\mu, \nu))$ of the model parameters, the maximum likelihood estimator of the s-year survival probability is

$$p(X_t, t, s; \theta) = E_\gamma \left(e^{-\int_t^{t+s}[\Lambda(X_u;\nu)+A(X_u;\mu)] \, du} \,\middle|\, X_t\right),$$

and the maximum likelihood estimator of the s-year default probability is

$$q(X_t, t, s; \theta) = E_\gamma \left(\int_t^{t+s} e^{-\int_t^{t+z}[\Lambda(X_u;\nu)+A(X_u;\mu)] \, du} A(X_z; \nu) \, dz \,\middle|\, X_t\right).$$

These expressions show the dependence of the default and censoring intensities on the intensity parameters μ and ν, respectively, and use "E_γ" to indicate the dependence of the expectation on the time-series parameter γ, which determines the probability distribution of the path of X.

Drawing from Section 2.4, one can now calculate the maximum likelihood estimator of the s-year default hazard rate as

$$h(X_t, t, s; \theta) = \frac{1}{p(X_t, t, s; \theta)} E_\gamma \left(e^{-\int_t^{t+s} [\Lambda(X_u; \nu) + A(X_u; \mu)] \, du} \Lambda(X_s; \nu) \, \bigg| \, X_t \right).$$

3.5 THE DISTRIBUTION OF ESTIMATORS

Although we do not develop a consistency result here, demonstrating that the parameter estimators converge with sample size to the true parameters could be based on allowing both the number k of observation periods and the number n of types of firms to become large. This remains for future work.

Under technical conditions, assuming consistency, the difference between the maximum likelihood estimator and the "true" data-generating parameter, appropriately scaled as the number of observations grows larger, converges weakly to a vector whose distribution is joint normal with mean zero and with a particular covariance matrix based on sample size. The asymptotic distribution of various properties of the parameter estimators can be computed from the so-called "Delta method," and then used for inference. Alternatively, in samples of a given size, Monte Carlo methods can be used to obtain estimates of the probability distribution of the estimators.

4

The Default Intensities of
Public Corporations

Using the econometric approach developed in Chapter 3, we now provide estimates of default intensities and term structures of default probabilities of U.S. non-financial firms, using data for 1979 to 2005. The results reported here are from Duffie, Saita, and Wang (2007) and Duffie, Eckner, Horel, and Saita (2009).

We will see that a firm's default probabilities depend heavily on the firm's distance to default, a volatility-adjusted leverage measure. The term structures of default probabilities reflect the tendency of public firms to target leverage as well as the mean reversion associated with the macroeconomic business cycle. The term structures of default hazard rates are typically upward-sloping at business-cycle peaks and downward sloping at business-cycle troughs, to a degree that depends on corporate leverage relative to its long-run target.

In principle, the estimated model can also be used to calculate probabilities of joint default of groups of firms, or other portfolio-based measures of default risk that depend on default correlation. In our doubly-stochastic model setting, the default correlation between firms arises from (i) common dependence of default intensities on macro-variables and (ii) correlation across firms of firm-specific covariates, such as leverage. In Chapter 5, however, will see that the model estimated in this chapter leads to substantial underestimation of the degree to which defaults are correlated. Chapters 6 and 7 therefore extend the model to handle additional unobservable sources of default correlation.

4.1 DATA

Our data, drawing from Bloomberg, Compustat, CRSP, and Moody's, was constructed by Duffie, Saita, and Wang (2007) and extended by Duffie, Eckner, Horel, and Saita (2009) through of an examination of The Directory of

Obsolete Securities and the SDC database for additional mergers, defaults, and failures. The small number of additional defaults and mergers identified through these sources do not materially change the default intensities estimated by Duffie, Saita, and Wang (2007).

The data on corporate defaults and bankruptcies are from two sources, Moody's Default Risk Service and CRSP/Compustat. Moody's Default Risk Service provides detailed issue and issuer information on rating, default, and bankruptcy date and type (for example, distressed exchange or missed interest payment), tracking 34,984 firms as of 1938. CRSP/Compustat provides reasons for deletion and year and month of deletion (data items AFTNT35, AFTNT34, and AFTNT33, respectively). Firm-specific financial data come from the CRSP/Compustat database. Stock prices are from CRSP's monthly file. Short-term and long-term debt levels are from Compustat's annual (data items DATA5, DATA9, and DATA34) and quarterly files (DATA45, DATA49, and DATA51), respectively. The S&P500 index trailing one-year returns are from monthly CRSP data. Treasury rates come from the web site of the U.S. Federal Reserve Board of Governors. Included firms are those in Moody's "Industrial" category sector for which there is a common firm identifier for the Moody's, CRSP, and Compustat databases. This includes essentially all matchable U.S.-listed non-financial non-utility firms. We restrict attention to firms for which we have at least six months of monthly data both in CRSP and Compustat. Because Compustat provides only quarterly and yearly data, for each month we take the accounting debt measures to be those provided for the corresponding quarter.

The data cover 402,434 firm-months spanning January 1979 through March 2004. Because of the manner in which defaults are defined, it is appropriate to use data only up to December 2003. For the total of 2,793 companies in this data set, Table 4.1 shows the number of firms in each exit category. Of the total of 496 defaults, 176 first occurred as bankruptcies, although many of the "other defaults" eventually led to bankruptcy.

The exit types are defined as follows.

- Bankruptcy.   An exit is treated for our purposes as a bankruptcy if coded in Moody's database under any of the following categories of events:

Table 4.1: Number of firm exits of each type.

Exit type	Number
bankruptcy	176
other default	320
Merger-acquisition	1,047
Other exit	671

Source: Duffie, Eckner, Horel, and Saita (2009).

Bankruptcy, Bankruptcy Section 77, Chapter 10,[1] Chapter 11, Chapter 7, and Prepackaged Chapter 11. A bankruptcy is also recorded if the record in data item AFTNT35 of Compustat is 2 or 3 (for Chapters 11 and 7, respectively). In some cases, our data reflect bankruptcy exits based on information from Bloomberg and other data sources.

- Other defaults. A default is defined as a bankruptcy, as above, or as any of the following additional default types in the Moody's database: distressed exchange, dividend omission, grace-period default, indenture modified, missed interest payment, missed principal and interest payments, missed principal payment, payment moratorium, suspension of payments. We also include any defaults recorded in Bloomberg or other data sources.

- Acquisition. Exits due to acquisitions and mergers are as recorded by Moody's, CRSP/Compustat, and Bloomberg.

- Other exits. Some firms are dropped from the CRSP/Compustat database or the Moody's database for other specified reasons, such as reverse acquisition, "no longer fits original file format," leveraged buyout, "now a private company," or "Other" (CRSP/Compustat AFTNT35 codes 4, 5, 6, 9, 10 respectively). We have also included in this category exits that are indicated in the Moody's database to be any of cross-default, conservatorship, placed under administration, seized by regulators, or receivership. We also include firms that are dropped from CRSP/Compustat for no stated reason (under item AFTNT35). When such a failure to include a firm continues for more than 180 days, we take the last observation date to be the exit date from our data set. Most of the other exits are due to data gaps of various types.

Moody's annual corporate bond default study[2] provides a detailed exposition of historical default rates for various categories of firms since 1920.

We rely heavily on a default intensity covariate known as the "distance to default," which is a volatility-adjusted measure of leverage. Our construction of the the distance to default covariate is along the lines of that used by Crosbie and Bohn (2002), Vassalou and Xing (2004), and Hillegeist, Keating, Cram, and Lundstedt (2004). Although this conventional approach to measuring distance to default involves some rough approximations, Bharath and Shumway (2008) provide evidence that default prediction is relatively robust to varying the proposed measure with some relatively simple alternatives. Motivated by the models of Black and Scholes (1973) and Merton (1974), the distance to default is, in theory, the number of standard deviations of annual asset growth by which assets exceed a measure of book liabilities. In order to construct

---

[1] Chapter 10 is limited to businesses engaged in commercial or business activities, not including real estate, whose aggregate debts do not exceed $2,500,000.
[2] Moody's Investor Service, "Historical Default Rates of Corporate Bond Issuers."

the distance to default covariate at time t, the market capitalization S_t of the firm's equity is first measured as the end-of-month stock price multiplied by the number of shares outstanding, from the CRSP database. The so-called "default point" L_t is an accounting-based liability measure defined as the sum of short-term debt and one-half long-term debt, as obtained from Compustat data.[3] The risk-free interest rate, r_t, is taken to be the current 3-month T-bill rate. One solves for the implied asset value A_t and asset volatility σ_A by iteratively[4] applying the equations:

$$S_t = A_t \Phi(d_1) - L_t e^{-r_t} \Phi(d_2)$$

$$\sigma_A = \widehat{\text{sdev}} \left(\log(A_i) - \log(A_{i-1}) \right),$$

where Φ is the standard normal cumulative distribution function, and d_1 and d_2 are defined by

$$d_1 = \frac{1}{\sigma_A} \left(\log \left(\frac{A_t}{L_t} \right) + \left(r_t + \frac{1}{2}\sigma_A^2 \right) \right)$$

$$d_2 = d_1 - \sigma_A.$$

We avoided estimating the asset volatility σ_A by a direct application of the Black-Scholes option pricing model (as suggested by Crosbie and Bohn (2002) and Hillegeist, Keating, Cram, and Lundstedt (2004)), instead estimating σ_A as the sample standard deviation of the historical time series of the growth rates of asset valuations. The distance to default can now be defined as

$$\delta_t = \frac{\ln \left(\frac{A_t}{L_t} \right) + \left(\mu_A - \frac{1}{2}\sigma_A^2 \right) T}{\sigma_A \sqrt{T}},$$

where μ_A is the firm's mean rate of asset growth and T is a chosen time horizon, in our case 4 quarters. As a simplifying approximation, we took μ_A to be the risk-free rate.

Figure 4.1 shows a frequency plot of measured levels of the distance-to-default for the entire sample of 402,434 firm-months. As illustrated, a small fraction of the sampled distances to default are negative, which occurs whenever a firm's market value of equity is sufficiently low relative to accounting liabilities.

Our base-case model of default intensities uses the following list of observable firm-specific and macroeconomic covariates:

---

[3] We have measured short term debt as the larger of Compustat items 45 ("Debt in current liabilities") and 49 ("Total Current Liabilities"). If these accounting measures of debt are missing in the Compustat quarterly file, but available in the annual file, we replace the missing data with the associated annual debt observation.

[4] This iterative procedure is initialized by taking $A_t = S_t + L_t$.

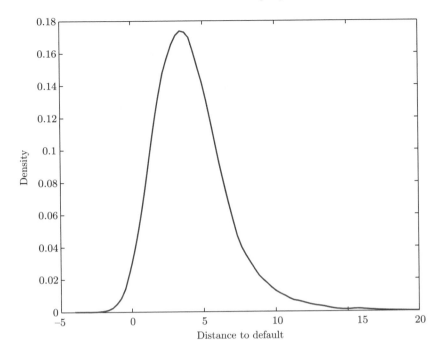

Fig. 4.1: Cross-sectional distribution of distance to default. Population density estimate of the measured levels of distance to default for the entire sample of 402,434 firm-months, between January 1979 and March 2004. The estimate was obtained by applying a Gaussian kernel smoother (bandwidth equal to 0.2) to the empirical distribution.

Source: Source: Duffie, Eckner, Horel, and Saita (2009).

- Distance to default.
- The firm's trailing 1-year stock return.
- The 3-month Treasury bill rate.
- The trailing 1-year return on the S&P 500 index.

4.2 COVARIATE TIME-SERIES SPECIFICATION

We summarize here the particular parameterization of the time-series model for the covariates. Because of the high-dimensional state vector, which includes the macroeconomic covariates as well as the distance to default and size of each of almost 3,000 firms, we have opted for a Gaussian first-order vector autoregressive time-series model, with the following simple structure.

The 3-month and 10-year treasury rates, r_{1t} and r_{2t}, respectively, are modeled by taking $r_t = (r_{1t}, r_{2t})'$ to satisfy

$$r_{t+1} = r_t + k_r(\theta_r - r_t) + C_r\epsilon_{t+1}, \qquad (4.1)$$

where $\epsilon_1, \epsilon_2, \ldots$ are independent standard-normal vectors, C_r is a 2×2 lower-triangular matrix, and the time step is one month. Provided C_r is of full rank, this is a simple arbitrage-free two-factor affine term-structure model.

For the distance to default D_{it} and log-assets V_{it} of firm i, and the trailing one-year S&P500 return, S_t, we assume that

$$\begin{bmatrix} D_{i,t+1} \\ V_{i,t+1} \end{bmatrix} = \begin{bmatrix} D_{it} \\ V_{it} \end{bmatrix} + \begin{bmatrix} k_D & 0 \\ 0 & k_V \end{bmatrix} \left(\begin{bmatrix} \theta_{iD} \\ \theta_{iV} \end{bmatrix} - \begin{bmatrix} D_{it} \\ V_{it} \end{bmatrix} \right)$$
$$+ \begin{bmatrix} b \cdot (\theta_r - r_t) \\ 0 \end{bmatrix} + \begin{bmatrix} \sigma_D & 0 \\ 0 & \sigma_V \end{bmatrix} \eta_{i,t+1}, \qquad (4.2)$$

$$S_{t+1} = S_t + k_S(\theta_S - S_t) + \xi_{t+1}, \qquad (4.3)$$

where

$$\eta_{it} = Az_{it} + Bw_t, \qquad (4.4)$$

$$\xi_t = \alpha_S u_t + \gamma_S w_t,$$

for $\{z_{1t}, z_{2t}, \ldots, z_{nt}, w_t : t \geq 1\}$ that are *iid* 2-dimensional standard-normal, all independent of $\{u_1, u_2, \ldots\}$, which are independent standard normals.[5] For simplicity, although this is unrealistic, we assume that ϵ is independent of (η, ξ). The maximum likelihood parameter estimates, with standard errors, are provided in Appendix A.

4.3 DEFAULT INTENSITY ESTIMATES

The default intensity of firm i at time t is assumed to be of the form

$$\lambda_i(t) = \exp\left(\beta_0 + \beta_1 U_{i1}(t) + \beta_2 U_{i2}(t) + \beta_3 Z_1(t) + \beta_4 Z_2(t)\right), \qquad (4.5)$$

where $U_{i1}(t)$ and $U_{i2}(t)$ are the distance to default and trailing stock return of firm i, $Z_1(t)$ is the U.S. 3-month Treasury bill rate, and $Z_2(t)$ is the trailing 1-year return of the Standard and Poors 500 stock index. Other-exit intensities

---

[5] The 2×2 matrices A and B have $A_{12} = B_{12} = 0$, and are normalized so that the diagonal elements of $AA' + BB'$ are 1. For estimation, some such standardization is necessary because the joint distribution of η_{it} (over all i) is determined by the 6 (non-unit) entries in $AA' + BB'$ and BB'. Our standardization makes A and B equal to the Cholesky decompositions of AA' and BB', respectively.

Table 4.2: Intensity parameter estimates. Maximum likelihood estimates of the intensity parameters. Estimated
asymptotic standard errors were computed using the
Hessian matrix of the likelihood function when evaluated
at the estimated parameters.

	Coefficient	Std. Error	*t*-statistic
Constant	−2.093	0.121	−17.4
Distance to default	−1.200	0.039	−30.8
Trailing stock return	−0.681	0.082	−8.3
3-month T-bill rate	−0.106	0.034	−3.1
Trailing S&P 500 return	1.481	0.997	1.5

Source: Duffie, Eckner, Horel, and Saita (2009).

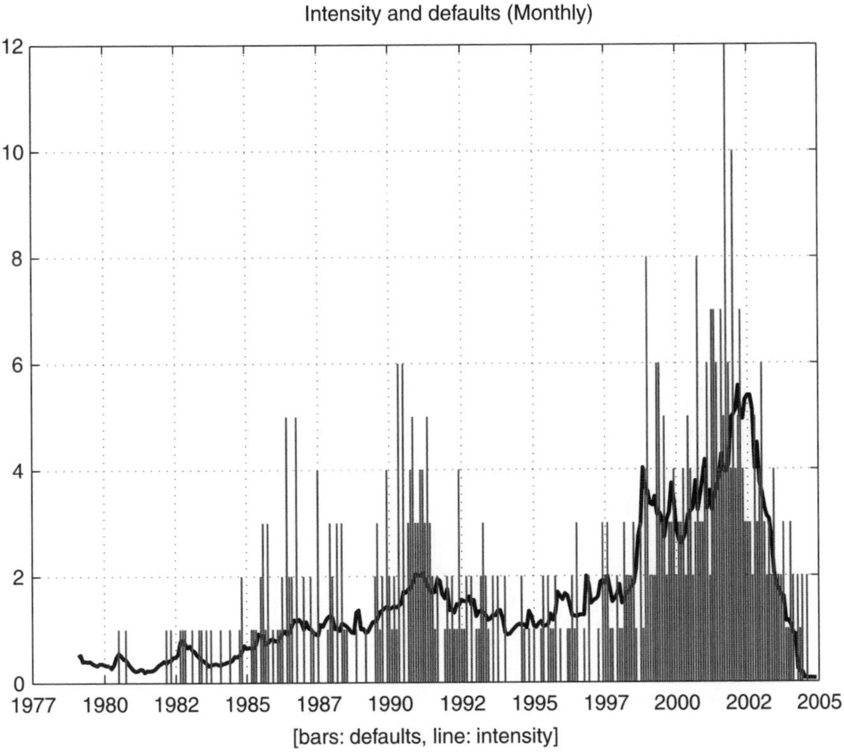

Intensity and defaults (Monthly)

[bars: defaults, line: intensity]

Fig. 4.2: Intensities and defaults. Aggregate (across firms) of monthly default intensities and number of defaults by month, from 1979 to 2004. The vertical bars represent
the number of defaults, and the line depicts the intensities.

Source: Das, Duffie, Kapadia, Saita (2007).

(for example due to merger or acquisition) are assumed to have the same parametric form as default intensities. Table 4.2 reports the estimates of the default intensity parameters β_0 through β_4. The coefficients determining the dependence of the other-exit intensities on the covariates, reported in Duffie, Saita, and Wang (2007), are not significantly different from zero, according to standard hypothesis tests. Although this represents a serious shortcoming of the model from the viewpoint of predicting the likelihood of other exits, it remains important to allow for the mean rate of other exits when estimating likelihoods of default, as we will illustrate at the end of the chapter.

Figure 4.2 illustrates the number of defaults, month by month, which ranges from a minimum of 0 to a maximum of 12, as well as a plot of the total across firms of the estimated monthly default intensities. (The plotted total intensity is actually that from Duffie, Saita, and Wang (2007) rather than Duffie, Eckner, Horel, and Saita (2009), but these are virtually identical.) By definition, if the default intensities are correctly measured, the number of defaults in a given month is a random variable whose conditional mean, given the total intensity path, is approximately equal to the average of the total intensity path for the month.

4.4 TERM STRUCTURES OF DEFAULT PROBABILITIES

We illustrate the results of the model with estimated term structures of default hazard rates for Xerox Incorporated. We start by taking the conditioning date t to be January 1, 2001. The corresponding estimated term structure of default hazard rates shown in Figure 4.3 is downward-sloping mainly because Xerox's distance to default at that time, 0.95, was well below its estimated target, $\hat{\theta}_{iD} = 4.4$ (which has an estimated standard error of 1.4). Other indications that Xerox was in significant financial distress at this point were its 5-year default swap rate of 980 basis points[6] and its trailing 1-year stock return[7] of -71%.

Figure 4.3 shows the hypothetical effects on the term structure of Xerox's default hazard rates of one-standard-deviation shifts (from its estimated stationary distribution) of its distance to default, above or below its current level.[8] In terms of both the impact of normalized shocks to default intensity as well time-series persistence, shocks to distance to default have much greater

---

[6] This CDS rate is an average of quotes provided from GFI and Lombard Risk.

[7] As an intensity covariate, the trailing-stock-return covariate is measured on a continuously compounding basis, and was -124%.

[8] For example, with a mean-reversion parameter of κ_Y and an innovation standard deviation of σ_Y, with maximum likelihood estimates of $\hat{\kappa}_Y$ and $\hat{\sigma}_Y$ respectively, the stationary distribution of a first-order autoregressive process Y has a variance whose maximum likelihood estimate is $\hat{\sigma}_Y^2/(1-(1-\hat{\kappa}_Y)^2)$.

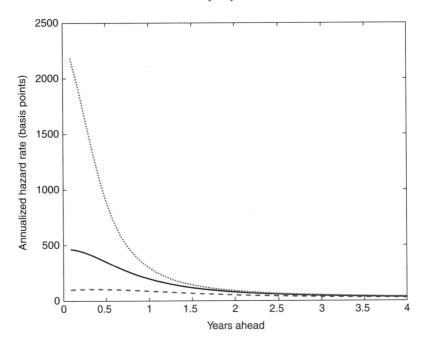

Fig. 4.3: Term structure of Xerox default hazard rates in 2001. Annualized Xerox default hazard rates as of January 1, 2001 (solid curve), and with distance to default at one standard deviation (1.33) below its current level of 0.95 (dotted curve), and with distance to default at one standard deviation above current level (dashed curve). The trailing S&P 500 return was −8.6%, the trailing 1-year stock return of Xerox was −71%, the 3-month Treasury rate was 5.8%, and the 10-year Treasury yield was 5.2%.

Source: Duffie, Saita, and Wang (2007).

effects on the term structure of Xerox's default hazard rates than do similarly significant shocks to any of the other covariates. The effect of such a shift in interest rates has a smaller effect than the effect of the analogous shift to Xerox's distance to default, both because of the relative sizes of these shocks, as scaled by the corresponding intensity coefficients, and also because interest rates are less persistent (have a higher mean-reversion rate) than distance to default.

As illustrated, the shapes of the term structure of Xerox's conditional default hazard rates reflect the time-series dynamics of the covariates. The counter-cyclical behavior of default probabilities is already well documented in such prior studies as Fons (1991), Blume and Keim (1991), Jonsson and Fridson (1996), McDonald and Van de Gucht (1999), Hillegeist, Keating, Cram, and Lundstedt (2004), Chava and Jarrow (2004), and Vassalou and Xing (2004). Our focus here is on the influence of firm-specific and macro-covariates on the likelihood of corporate default, not just during the immediately subsequent time period, but also for a number additional time periods into the future, incorporating the effects of mean reversion, volatilities, and correlation.

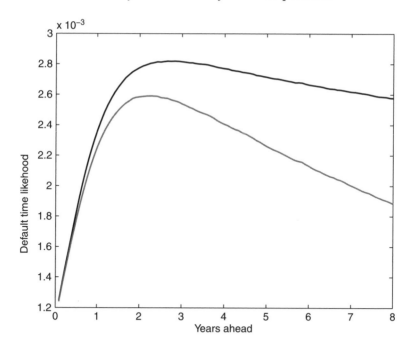

Fig. 4.4: Impact on default time density of other exits. Estimated conditional density of Xerox's default time as of January 1, 2004. Bottom plot: the estimated default time density, incorporating the impact of survival from merger and acquisition. Top plot: the estimated default-time density obtained by ignoring (setting to zero) the intensity of other exits.

Source: Duffie, Saita, and Wang (2007).

Figure 4.4 shows the estimated conditional probability density function of Xerox's default time, given by

$$\frac{d}{du} q(X_t, t, u),$$

where $q(X_t, t, u)$ is given by (2.7), for a conditioning date t of January 1, 2004. The figure also shows how much higher the default-time density would be if one were to ignore the effect of other exits such as merger and acquisition (that is, if one assumes that the other-exit intensity is zero). The figure illustrates the importance of adjusting estimates of default probabilities for the effects of other forms of exit. Xerox obviously cannot itself fail more than one year into the future in the event that it is merged with another firm in less than one year. In practice, there is of course concern over the risk of default of debt instruments that are assumed by an acquiring or merged firm, rather than paid upon merger.

5

Default Correlation

Default correlation, and more generally the manner in which defaults cluster in time, is central to the risk management of debt portfolios and to the design, pricing, and risk management of securitized credit products such as collateralized debt obligations. This chapter is devoted to a consideration of alternative sources of default correlation beyond the factors that are captured by measured intensities. The chapter includes a battery of tests indicating that the default intensities estimated in the previous chapter fail to capture a substantial amount of default correlation.

5.1 SOURCES OF DEFAULT CORRELATION

There are several channels for corporate default correlation. First, firms may be exposed to common or correlated risk factors whose co-movements cause correlated changes in their conditional default probabilities. Second, the event of default by one firm may be "contagious," in that one firm's default may directly worsen the economic environment of another, and thus push the other firm toward default. For example, the defaulting firm may have been a customer or supplier of the other firm. Third, the default of one firm may reveal previously hidden information that is relevant to the prospects of surviving firms. For example, to the extent that the defaults of Enron and WorldCom revealed accounting irregularities that could have been present in other firms, they may have had a direct impact on the conditional default probabilities of other firms.

Our primary objective in this chapter is to examine whether cross-firm default correlation that is associated with the observable factors used in Chapter 4 to determine conditional default probabilities, the first channel on its own, is sufficient to account for the degree of time clustering in defaults that we find in the data. Under the basic model of Chapter 4, default correlation can be fully attributed to co-movement across firms of the risk factors that determine the individual firms' default intensities. While this model is relatively tractable, we will see in this chapter, which is based entirely on Das et al. (2007), that the observable risk factors that we use here to measure default intensities lead to substantially less default correlation for U.S. public corporations during 1979–2005 than we actually find in the data. This will lead us to the "frailty" model explored in Chapters 6 and 7, which allows for unobserved sources of default correlation, that is, the third channel mentioned above.

We will not explore the second channel, of direct structural dependencies among firms, a source of default contagion whose presence is empirically estimated by Lando and Nielsen (2009) and Azizpour and Giesecke (2010) using a self-exciting intensity approach, in which default intensities react to default arrivals according to a specification whose parameters are estimated from the data. Lang and Stulz (1992) explore evidence of default contagion in equity prices. Jorion and Zhang (2007) find evidence of contagion through reactions in the pricing of credit default swaps to the defaults of related firms. Theoretical work on the impact of contagion on default pricing includes that of Davis and Lo (2001), Giesecke (2004), Jarrow et al. (2005), Kusuoka (1999), Schönbucher and Schubert (2001), Yu (2003), and Zhou (2001). Collin-Dufresne et al. (2010), Giesecke (2004), and Jarrow and Yu (2001), explore learning-from-default interpretations, based on the statistical modeling of frailty, according to which default intensities include the expected effect of unobservable covariates. In a frailty setting, the arrival of a default causes (via Bayes' Rule) a jump in the conditional distribution of hidden covariates, and therefore a jump in the conditional default probabilities of any other firms whose default intensities depend on the same unobservable covariates. Yu (2005) finds empirical evidence that, other things equal, a reduction in the measured precision of accounting variables is associated with a widening of credit spreads.

Understanding how corporate defaults are correlated is particularly important for the risk management of portfolios of corporate debt. For example, to back the performance of their loan portfolios, banks retain capital at levels designed to withstand default clustering at extremely high confidence levels, such as 99.9%. Some banks determine their capital requirements on the basis of models in which default correlation is assumed to be captured by common risk factors determining conditional default probabilities, as in Gordy (2003) and Vasicek (2004). If defaults are more heavily clustered in time than envisioned in these default risk models, then significantly greater capital might be required in order to survive default losses, especially at high confidence levels. An understanding of the sources and degree of default clustering is also crucial for the design, rating, and risk analysis of structured credit products, such as collateralized debt obligations (CDOs), that are exposed to loss once the total loss of the underlying portfolio of obligations exceeds a design threshold known as over-collateralization.

5.2 RESCALING TIME FOR POISSON DEFAULTS

In order to test whether estimated default intensities are likely to be missing some sources of default correlation, we consider a change of time-scale under which the passage of one unit of "new time" corresponds to a period of calendar time over which the cumulative total of all firms' default intensities increases by one unit. This is the calendar time period that, at current intensities, would include one default in expectation. Under this new time-scale, the cumulative number of defaults to date defines a standard (constant mean arrival rate) Poisson process. We will look for evidence that defaults arrive in patterns that are more clustered in time than suggested by the default intensities, after allowing appropriately for randomness.

Specifically, we exploit the following result, based on time rescaling suggested by Proposition 2 (Chapter 2).

Corollary to Proposition 2. *Consider the rescaling of time under which the passage of each additional unit of new time corresponds to the calendar period necessary to accumulate an additional unit of the total default intensity of all surviving firms. Let $J(s)$ be the number of defaults that have occurred by "new" (rescaled) time s. Under the no-simultaneous-defaults condition of Proposition 2, for any bin size $c > 0$, the numbers*

$$N_1 = J(c), \ N_2 = J(2c) - J(c), \ N_3 = J(3c) - J(2c), \ \dots$$

of defaults in successive time bins, each containing c units of rescaled time, are independent Poisson distributed random variables with mean c.

Tests based on this and other implications of Proposition 2 will be applied, as follows.

1. We apply a Fisher dispersion test for consistency of the empirical distribution of the numbers $N_1, \dots, N_k, \dots$ of defaults in successive time bins of a given accumulated intensity c, with the theoretical Poisson distribution of mean c. The null hypothesis that defaults arrive according to a time-changed Poisson process is rejected at traditional confidence levels for all of the bin sizes that we study (2, 4, 6, 8, and 10).

2. We test whether the mean of the upper quartile of our sample $N_1, N_2, \dots, N_K$ of numbers of defaults in successive time bins of a given size c is significantly larger than the mean of the upper quartile of a sample of like size drawn independently from the Poisson distribution with parameter c. An analogous test is based on the median of the upper quartile. These tests are designed to detect default clustering in excess of that implied by the default intensities. We also extend this test so as to simultaneously treat a number of bin sizes. The null is rejected at traditional confidence levels at

bin sizes 2, 4, and 10, and is rejected in a joint test covering all bins. That is, at least insofar as this test implies, the data suggest clustering of defaults in excess of that implied by the estimated intensities.

3. Taking another perspective, some of our tests are based on the fact that, in the new time-scale, the inter-arrival times of default are independent and identically distributed exponential variables with parameter 1. We provide the results of a test due to Prahl (1999) for clustering of default arrival times (in our new time-scale) in excess of that associated with a Poisson process. The null is rejected, which again provides evidence of clustering of defaults in excess of that suggested by the assumption that default correlation is captured by co-movement of the default covariates used for intensity estimation.

4. Fixing the size c of time bins, Appendix C.2 provides the results of tests of serial correlation of $N_1, N_2, \ldots$ by fitting an autoregressive model. The presence of serial correlation would imply a failure of the independent-increments property of Poisson processes, and, if the serial correlation were positive, could lead to default correlation in excess of that associated with the estimated default intensities. The null is rejected in favor of positive serial correlation for all bin sizes except $c = 2$.

Because these tests do not depend on the joint probability distribution of the firms' default intensity processes, including their correlation structure, they allow for both generality and robustness. The data are broadly inconsistent with the hypothesis that default correlation across firms is adequately captured by the measured intensities. This rejection could be due to misspecification associated with missing covariates. For example, if the true default intensities depend on macroeconomic variables that are not used to estimate the *measured* intensities, then even after the change of time-scale based on the measured intensities, the default times could be correlated. For instance, if the true default intensities decline with increasing gross domestic product (GDP) growth, even after controlling for the other covariates, then periods of low GDP growth would induce more clustering of defaults than would be predicted by the measured default intensities. Appendix C.2 provides mild evidence that U.S. industrial production (IP) growth is a missing covariate. Even after re-estimating intensities after including this covariate, however, we continue to reject the nulls associated with the above tests (albeit at slightly larger p-values). Lando and Nielsen (2009) augment the model with additional covariates and fail to reject the model of intensities, although with a somewhat smaller sample size.

We will also gauge the degree of default correlation that is not captured by the estimated default intensities. For this purpose, Appendix B reports a calibration of the data to the intensity-conditional copula model of Schönbucher and Schubert (2001). The associated intensity-conditional Gaussian copula

correlation parameter is a measure of the amount of additional default correlation that must be added, on top of the default correlation already implied
by co-movement in default intensities, in order to match the degree of default
clustering observed in the data. The estimated incremental copula correlation
parameters reported in Appendix B range from 1% to 4% depending on the
length of time window used. By comparison, Akhavein et al. (2005) estimate an
unconditional Gaussian copula correlation parameter of approximately 19.7%
within sectors and 14.4% across sectors, by calibration to empirical default correlations, that is, before "removing" the correlation associated with covariance
in default intensities. Although this is a rough comparison, it indicates that
default intensity correlation accounts for a large fraction, but not all, of the
default correlation.

5.3 GOODNESS-OF-FIT TESTS

The data, essentially identical to those described in Chapter 4, cover the
slightly different time period spanning from January, 1979 to August, 2004;
include 2,770 distinct firms and 495 defaults; and span 392,404 firm-months.
The intensity specification and estimation procedure are identical to those
described in Chapter 4. The coefficient estimates, reported in Duffie et al.
(2007), are similar to those reported in Chapter 4.

Having estimated the annualized default intensity λ_{it} for each firm i and each
date t (with λ_{it} taken to be constant within months), and letting $\tau(i)$ denote
the default time of firm i, we let $U(t) = \int_0^t \sum_{i=1}^n \lambda_{is} 1_{\{\tau(i) > s\}} \, ds$ be the total
accumulative default intensity of all surviving firms. In order to obtain time
bins that each contain c units of accumulative default intensity, we construct
calendar times $t_0, t_1, t_2, \ldots$ such that $t_0 = 0$ and $U(t_i) - U(t_{i-1}) = c$. We then
let $N_k = \sum_{i=1}^n 1_{\{t_k \leq \tau(i) < t_{k+1}\}}$ be the number of defaults in the k-th time bin.
Figure 5.1 illustrates the construction of time bins of size $c = 8$, restricting
attention to the years 1995–2001 in order to better illustrate the effect of binning
the defaults.

Table 5.1 presents a comparison of the empirical and theoretical moments
of the distribution of defaults per bin, for each of several bin sizes. Under
the Poisson distribution, $P(N_k = n) = \frac{e^{-c} c^n}{n!}$. The associated moments of N_k
are a mean and variance of c, a skewness of $c^{-0.5}$, and a kurtosis of $3 + c^{-1}$.
The actual bin sizes vary slightly from the integer bin sizes shown because of
granularity in the construction of the binning times $t_1, t_2, \ldots$. The approximate
match between a bin size and the associated sample mean $(N_1 + \cdots + N_K)/K$
of the number of defaults per bin offers some confirmation that the underlying default intensity data are reasonably well estimated. However, this is

Table 5.1: Empirical and theoretical moments. This table presents a comparison of empirical and theoretical moments for the distribution of defaults per bin. The number K of bin observations is shown in parentheses under the bin size. The upper-row moments are those of the theoretical Poisson distribution; the lower-row moments are the empirical counterparts.

Bin size	Mean	Variance	Skewness	Kurtosis
2	2.04	2.04	0.70	3.49
(230)	2.12	2.92	1.30	6.20
4	4.04	4.04	0.50	3.25
(116)	4.20	5.83	0.44	2.79
6	6.04	6.04	0.41	3.17
(77)	6.25	10.37	0.62	3.16
8	8.04	8.04	0.35	3.12
(58)	8.33	14.93	0.41	2.59
10	10.03	10.03	0.32	3.10
(46)	10.39	20.07	0.02	2.24

Source: Das, Duffie, Kapadia, and Saita (2007).

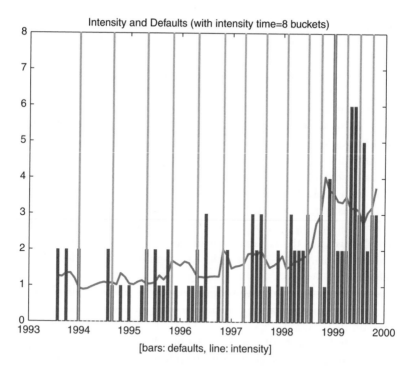

Fig. 5.1: Time rescaled intensity bins. Aggregate intensities and defaults by month, 1994–2000, with time bin delimiters marked for intervals that include a total accumulated default intensity of $c = 8$ per bin. The vertical bars represent the number of defaults in each month. The plotted line depicts the total of estimated default intensities.

Source: Das, Duffie, Kapadia, and Saita (2007).

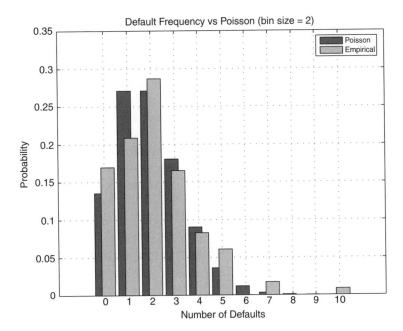

Fig. 5.2: Default distributions in small time bins. The empirical and theoretical distributions of defaults for bins of size 2. The theoretical distribution is Poisson.

Source: Das, Duffie, Kapadia, and Saita (2007).

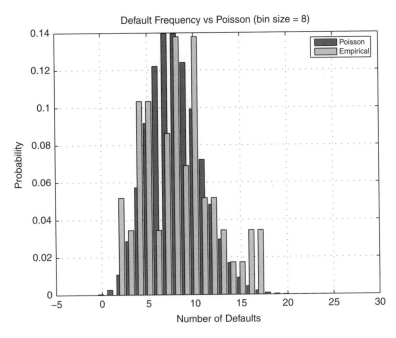

Fig. 5.3: Default distributions in large time bins. The empirical and theoretical distributions of defaults for bins of size 8. The theoretical distribution is Poisson.

Source: Das, Duffie, Kapadia, and Saita (2007).

somewhat expected given the within-sample nature of the estimates. The total number of defaults that is expected conditional on the paths of all default intensities is 470.6, whereas the actual number of defaults is 495. For larger bin sizes, Table 5.1 shows that the empirical variances are larger than their theoretical counterparts under the assumption of correctly estimated default intensities.

Figures 5.2 and 5.3 present the observed default frequency distribution and the associated theoretical Poisson distribution for bin sizes 2 and 8, respectively. To the extent that defaults depend on unobservable covariates, or at least on relevant covariates that are not included whether observable or not, violations of the Poisson distribution would tend to be larger for larger bin sizes because of the time necessary to build up a significant incremental impact of the missing covariates on the probability distribution of the number of defaults per bin.

5.3.1 Fisher's Dispersion Test

Our first goodness-of-fit test of the hypothesis of correctly measured default intensities is Fisher's dispersion test of the agreement of the empirical distribution of defaults per bin, for a given bin size c, to the theoretical Poisson distribution with parameter c.

Fixing the bin size c, a simple test of the null hypothesis that $N_1, \ldots, N_K$ are independent Poisson distributed variables with mean parameter c is Fisher's dispersion test, as described by Cochran (1954). Under this null,

$$W = \sum_{i=1}^{K} \frac{(N_i - c)^2}{c} \tag{5.1}$$

is approximately distributed as a χ^2 random variable with $K - 1$ degrees of freedom. An outcome for W that is large relative to a χ^2 random variable of the associated number of degrees of freedom would generate a small p-value, meaning a surprisingly large amount of clustering if the default intensities are well estimated. The p-values shown in Table 5.2 indicate that at standard confidence levels such as 95%, we reject this null hypothesis for all bin sizes.

5.3.2 Upper Tail Tests

If defaults are more positively correlated than would be suggested by the co-movement of intensities, then the upper tail of the empirical distribution of

Table 5.2: Fisher's dispersion test. The table presents Fisher's dispersion test for goodness of fit of the Poisson distribution with mean equal to bin size. Under the hypothesis that default intensities are correctly measured, the statistic W is χ^2-distributed with $K-1$ degrees of freedom.

Bin size	K	W	p-value
2	230	336.00	0.0000
4	116	168.75	0.0008
6	77	132.17	0.0001
8	58	107.12	0.0001
10	46	91.00	0.0001

Source: Das, Duffie, Kapadia, and Saita (2007).

defaults per bin could be fatter than that of the associated Poisson distribution. We use a Monte Carlo test of the "size" (mean or median) of the upper quartile of the empirical distribution against the theoretical size of the upper quartile of the Poisson distribution as follows.

For a given bin size c, we let M denote the sample mean of the upper quartile of the empirical distribution of $N_1, \ldots, N_K$, the numbers of defaults in the respective time bins. By Monte Carlo simulation, we generate 10,000 data sets, each consisting of K independent Poisson random variables with parameter c. The p-value is estimated as the fraction of the simulated data sets whose sample upper-quartile size (mean or median) is above the actual sample mean M. For four of the five bin sizes, the sample p-values presented in Table 5.3 suggest fatter upper-quartile tails than those of the theoretical Poisson distribution. That is, for these bins, our one-sided tests imply rejection of the null at typical confidence levels. The joint test across all bin sizes also implies a rejection of the null at standard confidence levels.

5.3.3 Prahl's Test of Clustered Defaults

Fisher's dispersion test and our tailored upper-tail tests do not efficiently exploit the information available across all bin sizes. In this section, we apply a test for "bursty" default arrivals due to Prahl (1999). Prahl's test is sensitive to clustering of arrivals in excess of those of a theoretical Poisson process. This test is particularly suited for detecting clustering of defaults that may arise from more default correlation than would be suggested by co-movement of default intensities alone. Prahl's test statistic is based on the fact that the inter-arrival times of a standard Poisson process are independent standard exponential

Table 5.3: Mean and median of default upper quartiles. This table presents tests of the mean and median of the upper quartile of defaults per bin against the associated theoretical Poisson distribution. The last row of the table, "All," indicates the estimated probability, under the hypothesis that time-changed default arrivals are Poisson with parameter 1, that there exists at least one bin size for which the mean (or median) of number of defaults per bin exceeds the corresponding empirical mean (or median).

Bin size	Mean of tails Data	Mean of tails Simulation	*p*-value	Median of tails Data	Median of tails Simulation	*p*-value
2	4.00	3.69	0.00	4.00	3.18	0.00
4	7.39	6.29	0.00	7.00	6.01	0.00
6	9.96	8.95	0.02	9.00	8.58	0.06
8	12.27	11.33	0.08	11.50	10.91	0.19
10	16.08	13.71	0.00	16.00	13.25	0.00
All			0.0018			0.0003

Source: Das, Duffie, Kapadia, and Saita (2007).

variables. Under the null, Prahl's test is therefore applied to determine whether, after the time change associated with aggregate default intensity accumulation, the inter-default times $Z_1, Z_2, \ldots$ are independent exponentially distributed random variables with parameter 1. (Because of data granularity, our mean is slightly smaller than 1.)

Table 5.4 provides the sample moments of inter-default times in the intensity-based time-scale. This table also presents the corresponding sample moments of the unscaled (actual calendar) inter-default times, after a linear scaling of time that matches the mean of the inter-default time distribution to that of the intensity-based time-scale. A comparison of the moments indicates that conditioning on intensities removes a large amount of default correlation, in the sense that the moments of the inter-arrival times in the default-intensity time-scale are much closer to the corresponding exponential moments than are those of the actual (calendar) inter-default times.

Letting C^* denote the sample mean of $Z_1, \ldots, Z_n$, Prahl shows that

$$M = \frac{1}{n} \sum_{\{k : Z_k < C^*\}} \left(1 - \frac{Z_k}{C^*}\right) \tag{5.2}$$

is asymptotically (in n) normally distributed with mean $\mu_n = e^{-1} - \alpha/n$ and variance $\sigma_n^2 = \beta^2/n$, where

Table 5.4: Moments of the distribution of inter-default times. This table presents selected moments of the distribution of inter-default times. For correctly measured default intensities, the inter-default times, measured in intensity-based time units, are exponentially distributed. The inter-arrival time empirical distribution is also shown in calendar time, after a linear scaling of time that matches the first moment, mean inter-arrival time.

Moment	Intensity time	Calendar time	Exponential
Mean	0.95	0.95	0.95
Variance	1.17	4.15	0.89
Skewness	2.25	8.59	2.00
Kurtosis	10.06	101.90	6.00

Source: Das, Duffie, Kapadia, and Saita (2007).

$$\alpha \simeq 0.189$$

$$\beta \simeq 0.2427.$$

Using our data, for $n = 495$ default times,

$$M = 0.4055$$

$$\mu_n = \frac{1}{e} - \frac{\alpha}{n} = 0.3675$$

$$\sigma_n = \frac{\beta}{\sqrt{n}} = 0.0109.$$

The test statistic M measured from our data is 3.48 standard deviations from the asymptotic mean associated with the null hypothesis of *iid* exponential inter-default times. This is evidence of default clustering significantly in excess of that associated with the measured default intensities. (In the calendar time-scale, the same test statistic M is 11.53 standard deviations from the mean μ_n under the null of exponential inter-default times.)

Figure 5.4 shows the empirical distribution of inter-default times before and after rescaling time in units of cumulative total default intensity, compared to the exponential density.[1]

[1] Das, Duffie, Kapadia, and Saita (2007) also report a Kolmogorov–Smirnov (KS) test of goodness of fit of the exponential distribution of inter-default times in the new time-scale. The associated KS statistic is 3.14 (which is $\sqrt{n}$ times the usual D statistic, where n is the number of default arrivals), for a p-value of 0.000, leading to a rejection of the hypothesis of correctly measured default intensities. (In calendar time, the corresponding KS statistic is 4.03.)

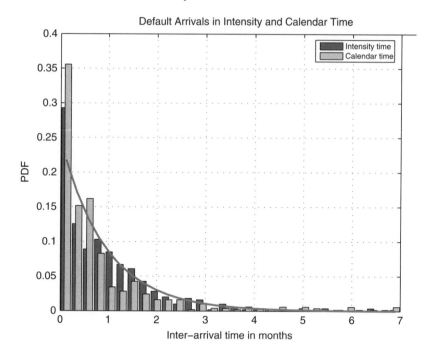

Fig. 5.4: Distribution of rescaled inter-default times. The empirical distribution of inter-default times after scaling time change by total intensity of defaults, compared to the theoretical exponential density. The distribution of default inter-arrival times is provided both in calendar time and in intensity time. The line depicts the theoretical probability density function for the inter-arrival times of default under the null of an exponential distribution.

Source: Das, Duffie, Kapadia, and Saita (2007).

5.4 DISCUSSION

Our results here present serious concerns regarding the ability of commonly applied credit risk models to capture the tails of the probability distribution of portfolio default losses, and may therefore be of particular interest to bank risk managers and regulators. For example, the level of economic capital necessary to support levered portfolios of corporate debt at high confidence levels is heavily dependent on the degree to which default intensities are measured well, and in particular whether they include most of the relevant sources of default correlation. This may be of special interest for quantitative portfolio credit risk analysis applied to bank capital regulations arising under international accords on regulatory capital (as in Allen and Saunders (2003) and Gordy (2003)). The challenge to develop more realistic models of default correlation is picked up in the last two chapters.

In new work, Lando and Nielsen (2009) have failed to reject a number of the tests reported in this chapter after augmenting the intensity model used here with several new covariates, the most powerful of which is an accounting measure of a firm's short-term indebtedness. (Their sample size is somewhat smaller than that used here.) Their improved intensity specification would likely be the basis for a superior model of portfolio default risk once coupled with a time-series model for the stochastic behavior of the covariates.

6

Frailty-Induced Correlation*

This chapter, based on Duffie, Eckner, Horel, and Saita (2009), provides a frailty-based model of joint default risk, by which firms have an unobservable common source of default risk that changes randomly over time. The posterior distribution of this frailty factor, conditional on past observable covariates and past defaults, represents a significant additional source of default correlation. For U.S. non-financial public firms during 1979–2004, the empirical evidence provided with this model, shown in the next chapter, indicates that frailty induces a large increase in default clustering, and significant additional fluctuation over time in the conditional expected level of default losses, above and beyond that predicted by our observable default covariates, including leverage, volatility, stock returns, and interest rates. Out-of-sample tests suggest that a model with frailty gives a more accurate assessment of the likelihood of major losses to a portfolio of corporate debt obligations.

Under the standard doubly-stochastic model described in Chapter 2 and estimated in Chapter 4, different firms' default times are correlated only to the extent implied by the correlation of observable factors determining their default intensities. The doubly-stochastic assumption significantly reduces the computational burden of the estimation. Chapter 5, however, provides evidence that defaults are significantly more correlated than suggested by the joint distribution of the default intensities estimated from only our observable covariates.

The doubly-stochastic assumption is violated in the presence of "frailty," meaning unobservable explanatory variables that may be correlated across firms. Even if all relevant covariates are observable in principle, some will inevitably be ignored in practice. The impacts of missing and unobservable covariates are essentially equivalent from the viewpoint of estimating default probabilities or portfolio credit risk.

* This chapter is based on Duffie, D., A. Eckner, G. Horel, and L. Saita (2009), Frailty Correlated Default, *Journal of Finance* 64, 2089–2123, Wiley-Blackwell.

Section 6.1 specifies a frailty-based model for the joint probability distribution of default times. Section 6.2 shows how to estimate the model parameters using a combination of the Monte Carlo EM algorithm and the Gibbs sampler. Chapter 7 summarizes some of the properties of the fitted model and of the posterior distribution of the frailty variable, given the entire sample.

6.1 THE FRAILTY MODEL

We fix a probability space $(\Omega, \mathcal{F}, P)$ and an information filtration $\{\mathcal{G}_t : t \geq 0\}$. A Markov state vector X_t contains firm-specific and macroeconomic covariates, but is only partially observable, in a sense to be defined. If all of these covariates were observable, the default intensity of firm i at time t would be of the form $\lambda_{it} = \Lambda_i(X_t, \beta)$, where β is a parameter vector to be estimated.

There are several channels by which the excessive default correlation shown in Chapter 5 could arise. With contagion, for example, default by one firm could have a direct influence on the default likelihood of another firm. This would be anticipated to some degree if one firm plays a relatively large role in the marketplace of another. The influence of the bankruptcy of auto parts manufacturer Delphi in November 2005 on the survival prospects of General Motors illustrates how failure by one firm could weaken another, above and beyond the default correlation associated with common or correlated covariates. Lando and Nielsen (2009) and Azizpour and Giesecke (2010) examine the data for evidence of a "self-exciting" effect, by which default intensities react immediately to defaults of other firms, according to a specified formula whose parameters are estimated from the data.

We examine instead the implications of "frailty," by which many firms could be jointly exposed to one or more unobservable risk factors. We restrict attention for simplicity to a single common frailty factor and to firm-by-firm idiosyncratic frailty factors, although a richer model and sufficient data could allow for the estimation of additional frailty factors, for example at the sectoral level.

The mathematical model that we adopt is actually doubly stochastic once the information available to the econometrician is artificially enriched to include the frailty factors. That is, conditional on the future paths of both the observable and unobservable components of the state vector X, firms are assumed to default independently. This implies two channels for default correlation: *(i)* future co-movement of the observable and unobservable factors determining intensities, and *(ii)* uncertainty regarding the current levels of unobservable covariates, after conditioning on past observations of the observable covariates and past defaults.

We let U_{it} be a firm-specific vector of covariates that are observable for firm i. We let V_t denote a vector of macroconomic variables that are observable at all times, and let Y_t be a vector of unobservable frailty variables. The complete state vector is then $X_t = (U_{1t}, \ldots, U_{mt}, V_t, Y_t)$, where m is the total number of firms in the data set.

We let $W_{it} = (1, U_{it}, V_t)$ be the vector of observed covariates for company i (including a constant). Since we observe these covariates on a monthly basis but measure default times continuously, we take $W_{it} = W_{i,k(t)}$, where $k(t)$ is the time of the most recent month end. We let T_i be the last observation time of company i, which could be the time of a default or another form of exit. While we take the first appearance time t_i to be deterministic, we could generalize and allow t_i to be a stopping time under regularity conditions.

The information filtration $(\mathcal{U}_t)_{0 \leq t \leq T}$ generated by firm-specific covariates is defined by

$$\mathcal{U}_t = \sigma \left(\{ U_{i,s} : 1 \leq i \leq m, t_i \leq s \leq t \wedge T_i \} \right).$$

The default-time filtration $(\mathcal{H}_t)_{0 \leq t \leq T}$ is given by

$$\mathcal{H}_t = \sigma \left(\{ D_{is} : 1 \leq i \leq m, t_i \leq s \leq t \wedge T_i \} \right),$$

where D_i is the default indicator process of company i (which is 0 before default, 1 afterwards). The econometrician's information filtration $(\mathcal{F}_t)_{0 \leq t \leq T}$ is defined by the join,

$$\mathcal{F}_t = \sigma \left(\mathcal{H}_t \cup \mathcal{U}_t \cup \{ V_s : 0 \leq s \leq t \} \right).$$

The complete-information filtration $(\mathcal{G}_t)_{0 \leq t \leq T}$ is the yet larger join

$$\mathcal{G}_t = \sigma \left(\{ Y_s : 0 \leq s \leq t \} \right) \vee \mathcal{F}_t.$$

With respect to the complete information filtration $(\mathcal{G}_t)$, default times and other exit times are assumed to be doubly stochastic, with the default intensity of firm i given by $\lambda_{it} = \Lambda(W_{it}, Y_t; \beta)$, where

$$\Lambda \left((w, y) ; \beta \right) = e^{v_1 w_1 + \cdots + v_n w_n + \eta y}, \tag{6.1}$$

for a parameter vector $\beta = (v, \eta, \kappa)$ common to all firms, where κ is a parameter whose role will be defined below. We can write

$$\lambda_{it} = e^{v \cdot W_{it}} e^{\eta Y_t} \equiv \tilde{\lambda}_{it} e^{\eta Y_t}, \tag{6.2}$$

so that $\tilde{\lambda}_{it}$ is the component of the $(\mathcal{G}_t)$-intensity that is due to observable covariates and $e^{\eta Y_t}$ is a scaling factor due to the unobservable frailty.

In the sense of Proposition 4.8.4 of Jacobsen (2006), the econometrician's default intensity for firm i is

$$\bar{\lambda}_{it} = E\left(\lambda_{it} \mid \mathcal{F}_t\right) = e^{v \cdot W_{it}} E\left(e^{\eta Y_t} \mid \mathcal{F}_t\right).$$

It is *not* generally true that the conditional probability of survival to a future time T (neglecting the effect of mergers and other exits) is given by the "usual formula"

$$E\left(e^{-\int_t^T \bar{\lambda}_{is}\, ds} \mid \mathcal{F}_t\right).$$

Rather, for a firm that has survived to time t, the probability of survival to time T (again neglecting other exits) is

$$P(\tau_i > T \mid \mathcal{F}_t) = E[P(\tau_i > T \mid \mathcal{G}_t) \mid \mathcal{F}_t] = E\left(e^{-\int_t^T \lambda_{is}\, ds} \mid \mathcal{F}_t\right), \qquad (6.3)$$

using the law of iterated expectations and the $\mathcal{G}_t$-conditional survival probability, $E\left(e^{-\int_t^T \lambda_{is}\, ds} \mid \mathcal{G}_t\right)$. Extending (6.3), the $\mathcal{F}_t$-conditional probability of joint survival by any subset A of currently alive firms until a future time T (ignoring other exits) is

$$E\left(e^{-\int_t^T \sum_{i \in A} \lambda_{is}\, ds} \mid \mathcal{F}_t\right).$$

We allow for censoring by other exits in the manner described in Chapter 3.

To further simplify notation, let $W = (W_1, \ldots, W_m)$ denote the vector of observed covariate processes for all companies, whose time-series behavior is determined by a parameter vector γ. We let $D = (D_1, \ldots, D_m)$ denote the vector of default indicators of all companies. That is, $D_{it} = 1_{\{\tau_i \leq t\}}$. On the complete-information filtration $(\mathcal{G}_t)$, the doubly-stochastic property and Proposition 3 (Chapter 3) imply that the likelihood of the data at the parameters (γ, β) is of the form

$$\mathcal{L}(\gamma, \beta \mid W, Y, D)$$

$$= \mathcal{L}(\gamma \mid W)\, \mathcal{L}(\beta \mid W, Y, D)$$

$$= \mathcal{L}(\gamma \mid W) \prod_{i=1}^{m} \left(e^{-\sum_{t=t_i}^{T_i} \lambda_{it} \Delta t} \prod_{t=t_i}^{T_i} [D_{it} \lambda_{it} \Delta t + (1 - D_{it})] \right). \qquad (6.4)$$

We simplify by supposing that the frailty process Y is independent of the observable covariate process W. With respect to the econometrician's filtration $(\mathcal{F}_t)$, the likelihood is therefore

$$\mathcal{L}(\gamma, \beta \mid W, D) = \int \mathcal{L}(\gamma, \beta \mid W, y, D) \, p_Y(y) \, dy$$

$$= \mathcal{L}(\gamma \mid W) \int \mathcal{L}(\beta \mid W, y, D) \, p_Y(y) \, dy$$

$$= \mathcal{L}(\gamma \mid W) E \left[\prod_{i=1}^{m} \left(e^{-\sum_{t=t_i}^{T_i} \lambda_{it} \Delta t} \prod_{t=t_i}^{T_i} [D_{it} \lambda_{it} \Delta t + (1 - D_{it})] \right) \,\middle|\, W, D \right],$$

$$(6.5)$$

where $p_Y(\cdot)$ is the unconditional probability density of the path of the unobserved frailty process Y. The final expectation of (6.5) is with respect to that density.[1]

Extending from Proposition 3 of Chapter 3, we can decompose this MLE problem into separate maximum likelihood estimations of γ and β, by maximization of the first and second factors on the right-hand side of (6.5), respectively.

In order to evaluate the expectation in (6.5), one could simulate sample paths of the frailty process Y. Since our covariate data are monthly observations from 1979 to 2004, evaluating (6.5) by direct simulation would call for Monte Carlo integration in a high-dimensional space. This is extremely numerically intensive by brute force Monte Carlo, given the overlying search for parameters. We now address a version of the model that can be feasibly estimated.

We suppose that Y is an Ornstein–Uhlenbeck (OU) process, in that

$$dY_t = -\kappa Y_t \, dt + dB_t, \qquad Y_0 = 0, \tag{6.6}$$

where B is a standard Brownian motion with respect to $(\Omega, \mathcal{F}, P, (\mathcal{G}_t))$, and where κ is a non-negative constant, the mean-reversion rate of Y. Without loss of generality, we have fixed the volatility parameter of the Brownian motion to be unity because scaling the parameter η, which determines via (6.1) the dependence of the default intensities on Y_t, plays precisely the same role in the model as scaling the frailty process Y.

Although an OU-process is a reasonable starting model for the frailty process, one could allow a richer model. We have found, however, that even our relatively large data set is too limited to identify much of the time-series properties of the frailty process. For the same reason, we have not attempted to identify sector-specific frailty effects.

---

[1] For notational simplicity, expression (6.5) ignores the precise intra-month timing of default, although it was accounted for in the parameter estimation by replacing Δt with $\tau_i - t_{i-1}$ in case that company i defaults in the time interval $(t_{i-1}, t_i]$.

The starting value and long-run mean of the OU-process are taken to be zero, since any change (of the same magnitude) of these two parameters can be absorbed into the default intensity intercept coefficient ν_1. However, we do lose some generality by taking the initial condition for Y to be deterministic and to be equal to the long-run mean. An alternative would be to add one or more additional parameters specifying the initial probability distribution of Y. We have found that the posterior of Y_t tends to be robust to the assumed initial distribution of Y, for points in time t that are a year or two after the initial date of our sample.

It may be that a substantial portion of the differences among firms' default risks is due to unobserved heterogeneity. Appendix F extends and estimates the model after introducing a firm-specific heterogeneity factor for firm i, in that the complete-information $(\mathcal{G}_t)$ default intensity of firm i is of the form

$$\lambda_{it} = Z_i \, e^{\nu \cdot W_{it}} \, e^{\eta Y_t} \tag{6.7}$$

where $Z_1, \ldots, Z_m$ are independently and identically gamma-distributed[2] random variables that are jointly independent of the observable covariates W and the common frailty process Y.

Fixing the mean of the heterogeneity factor Z_i to be 1 without loss of generality, we find that maximum likelihood estimation does not pin down the variance of Z_i to any reasonable precision with our limited set of data. We anticipate that far larger data sets would be needed, given the already large degree of observable heterogeneity and the fact that default is, on average, relatively unlikely. In the end, we examine the potential role of unobserved heterogeneity for default risk by fixing the standard deviation of Z_i at 0.5. The likelihood function is again given by (6.5).

6.2 PARAMETER ESTIMATION

We now turn to the problem of inference from data. The parameter vector γ determining the time-series model of the observable covariate process W is as specified and estimated in Chapter 4 and Appendix A. This model is vector-autoregressive Gaussian, with a number of structural restrictions chosen for parsimony and tractability. We focus here on the estimation of the parameter vector β of the default intensity model.

---

[2] Pickles and Crouchery (1995) show in simulation studies that it is relatively safe to make concrete parametric assumptions about the distribution of frailty variables. Inference is expected to be similar whether the frailty distribution is modeled as gamma, log-normal or some other parametric family, but for analytical tractability we chose the gamma distribution.

We use a variant of the expectation-maximization (EM) algorithm of Demptser, Laird, and Rubin (1977), an iterative method for the computation of the maximum likelihood estimator of parameters of models involving missing or incomplete data.[3]

Maximum likelihood estimation of the intensity parameter vector β with our variant of the EM algorithm involves the following steps:

0. Initialize an estimate of $\beta = (\nu, \eta, \kappa)$ at $\beta^{(0)} = (\widehat{\nu}, 0.05, 0)$, where $\widehat{\nu}$ is the maximum likelihood estimator of ν in the model without frailty, which can be obtained by maximizing the likelihood function (6.4) by standard methods such as the Newton–Raphson algorithm.

1. (E-step) Given the current parameter estimate $\beta^{(k)}$ and the observed covariate and default data W and D, respectively, draw n independent sample paths $Y^{(1)}, \ldots, Y^{(n)}$ from the conditional density $p_Y(\cdot \mid W, D, \beta^{(k)})$ of the latent Ornstein–Uhlenbeck frailty process Y using the Gibbs sampler described in Appendix D. We let

$$Q\left(\beta, \beta^{(k)}\right) = E_{\beta^{(k)}} \left(\log \mathcal{L}\left(\beta \mid W, Y, D\right)\right)$$

$$= \int \log \mathcal{L}\left(\beta \mid W, y, D\right) p_Y\left(y \mid W, D, \beta^{(k)}\right) dy,$$

where E_β denotes expectation with respect to the probability measure associated with a particular parameter vector β. This "expected complete-data log likelihood" or "intermediate quantity," as it is commonly called in the EM literature, can be approximated with the sample paths generated by the Gibbs sampler as

$$\widehat{Q}\left(\beta, \beta^{(k)}\right) = \frac{1}{n} \sum_{j=1}^{n} \log \mathcal{L}\left(\beta \mid W, Y^{(j)}, D\right). \tag{6.8}$$

2. (M-step) Maximize $\widehat{Q}(\beta, \beta^{(k)})$ with respect to the parameter vector β, for example by Newton–Raphson. The maximizing choice of β is the new parameter estimate $\beta^{(k+1)}$.

3. Replace k with $k+1$, and return to Step 1, repeating the E-step and the M-step until reasonable numerical convergence is achieved.

---

[3] See also Cappé, Moulines, and Rydén (2005), who discuss EM in the context of hidden Markov models. In many potential applications, explicitly calculating the conditional expectation required in the "E-step" of the algorithm may not be possible. Nevertheless, the expectation can be approximated by Monte Carlo integration, which gives rise to the stochastic EM algorithm, as explained for example by Celeux and Diebolt (1986) and Nielsen (2000), or to the Monte Carlo EM algorithm (Wei and Tanner 1990).

One can show[4] that $\mathcal{L}(\gamma, \beta^{(k+1)} \mid W, D) \geq \mathcal{L}(\gamma, \beta^{(k)} \mid W, D)$. That is, the observed data likelihood (6.5) is non-decreasing in each step of the EM algorithm. Under regularity conditions, the parameter sequence $\{\beta^{(k)} : k \geq 0\}$ therefore converges to at least a local maximum. (Wu (1983) provides a precise formulation of this convergence in terms of stationarity points of the likelihood function.) Nielsen (2000) gives sufficient conditions for global convergence and asymptotic normality of the parameter estimates, although these conditions are usually hard to verify in practice. As with many maximization algorithms, a simple way to mitigate the risk that one misses the global maximum is to start the iterations at many points throughout the parameter space.

Under regularity conditions, the Fisher and Louis identities (for example, Proposition 10.1.6 of Cappé, Moulines, and Rydén (2005)) imply the Jacobian

$$\nabla_\beta \mathcal{L}\left(\hat{\beta} \mid W, Y, D\right) = \nabla_\beta Q\left(\beta, \hat{\beta}\right)\big|_{\beta = \hat{\beta}}$$

and the Hessian

$$\nabla_\beta^2 \mathcal{L}\left(\hat{\beta} \mid W, Y, D\right) = \nabla_\beta^2 Q\left(\beta, \hat{\beta}\right)\big|_{\beta = \hat{\beta}}.$$

The Hessian matrix of the expected complete-data likelihood (6.8) can therefore be used to estimate asymptotic standard errors for the MLE parameter estimators.

Appendix F provides a generalization of the algorithm that incorporates unobserved heterogeneity.

The calculations necessary to produce the posterior probability distributions of the frailty process shown in the next chapter are based on the standard approach to filtering and smoothing in non-Gaussian state-space models, the so-called forward–backward algorithm due to Baum, Petrie, Soules, and Weiss (1970). For this, we let $R(t) = \{i : D_{i,t} = 0, t_i \leq t \leq T_i\}$ denote the set of firms that are alive at time t, and $\Delta R(t) = \{i \in R(t-1) : D_{it} = 1, t_i \leq t \leq T_i\}$ be the set of firms that defaulted at time t. A discrete-time approximation of the complete-information likelihood of the observed survivals and defaults at time t is

$$\mathcal{L}_t(\beta \mid W, Y, D) = \mathcal{L}_t(\beta \mid W_t, Y_t, D_t) = \prod_{i \in R(t)} e^{-\lambda_{it}\Delta t} \prod_{i \in \Delta R(t)} \lambda_{it}\Delta t.$$

Without mean reversion of the frailty process (that is, for $\kappa = 0$), the normalized version of the forward–backward algorithm allows us to calculate the filtered density of the latent Ornstein–Uhlenbeck frailty variable by the recursion

---

[4] For this, see Demptser, Laird, and Rubin (1977) or Gelman, Carlin, Stern, and Rubin (2004).

$$c_t = \int \int p\left(y_{t-1} \mid \mathcal{F}_{t-1}\right) \phi\left(y_t - y_{t-1}\right) \mathcal{L}_t\left(\beta \mid W_t, y_t, D_t\right) dy_{t-1} \, dy_t$$

$$p\left(y_t \mid \mathcal{F}_t\right) = \frac{1}{c_t} \int p\left(y_{t-1} \mid \mathcal{F}_{t-1}\right) p\left(y_t \mid y_{t-1}, \beta\right) \mathcal{L}_t\left(\beta \mid W_t, y_t, D_t\right) dy_{t-1},$$

where $\phi(\cdot)$ is the standard-normal density and $p\left(Y_t \mid Y_{t-1}, \beta\right)$ is the one-step transition density of the OU-process (6.6). For this recursion, we begin with the distribution (Dirac measure) of Y_0 concentrated at 0. For non-zero κ, we used a slight variant of this algorithm.

Once the filtered density $p\left(y_t \mid \mathcal{F}_t\right)$ is available, the marginal smoothed density $p\left(y_t \mid \mathcal{F}_T\right)$ can be calculated using the normalized backward recursions (as in Rabiner (1989)). Specifically, for $t = T - 1, T - 2, \ldots, 1$, we apply the recursion for the marginal density

$$\bar{\alpha}_{t|T}\left(y_t\right) = \frac{1}{c_{t+1}} \int p\left(y_t \mid y_{t-1}, \beta\right) \mathcal{L}_{t+1}\left(\beta \mid W_{t+1}, y_{t+1}, D_{t+1}\right) \bar{\alpha}_{t+1|T}\left(y_{t+1}\right) dy_{t+1}$$

$$p\left(y_t \mid \mathcal{F}_T\right) = p\left(y_t \mid \mathcal{F}_t\right) \bar{\alpha}_{t|T}\left(y_t\right),$$

beginning with $\bar{\alpha}_{T|T}\left(y_t\right) = 1$.

In order to explore the joint posterior distribution $p\left(\left(y_0, y_1, \ldots, y_T\right)' \mid \mathcal{F}_T\right)$ of the latent frailty variable, one could employ, for example, the Gibbs sampler described in Appendix D.

7

Empirical Evidence of Frailty*

This chapter, based on Duffie, Eckner, Horel, and Saita (2009), provides empirical evidence regarding the frailty-based model of correlated default risk described in Chapter 6. We also compare the fit of the model with some alternative specifications, mainly in order to address the robustness of our basic specification.

Our primary objective is to measure the degree of frailty that has been present for U.S. corporate defaults, and then to examine its empirical implications, especially for the risk of large total losses on corporate debt portfolios. We find strong evidence of persistent unobserved covariates. For example, even after controlling for the usual-suspect covariates, both firm-specific and macroeconomic, we find that defaults were persistently higher than expected during lengthy periods of time, for example 1986–1991, and persistently lower in others, for example during the mid-1990s. From trough to peak, the estimated impact of frailty on the average default rate of U.S. corporations during 1979–2005 is roughly a factor of 3. This is quite distinct from the effect of time fixed effects (time dummy variables, or baseline hazard functions), because of the discipline placed on the time-series behavior of the unobservable covariate through its transition probabilities, and because of the impact on portfolio loss risk of the common exposure of firms to the uncertain frailty variable. Deterministic time effects eliminate two important potential channels for default correlation, namely uncertainty regarding the current level of the time effect, and uncertainty regarding its future evolution.

Incorporating unobserved covariates also has an impact on the relative default probabilities of individual issuers because it changes the relative weights placed on different observable covariates, although this effect is not especially large for our data because of the dominant role of a single covariate, the "distance to default," the volatility-adjusted leverage measure defined in Chapter 4.

---

* This chapter is based on Duffie, D., A. Eckner, G. Horel, and L. Saita (2009), Frailty Correlated Default, *Journal of Finance* 64, 2089–2123, Wiley–Blackwell.

Section 7.1 provides the fitted model. Section 7.2 characterizes the posterior of the frailty variable at any point in time, given only past history. Section 7.3 illustrates the impact of frailty on estimates of the term structures of default probabilities of a given firm. Sections 7.4 and 7.5 provide an analysis of the impact of the frailty variable on default correlation and on the tail risk of a U.S. corporate debt portfolio. Section 7.6 examines the out-of-sample default prediction performance of our model, while Section 7.7 concludes and suggests some areas for future research.

Appendices F, G, and H, respectively, examine the impacts on the results of allowing for additional sources of unobserved variation across firms of default intensities, of allowing for unrestricted non-linear dependence of default intensities on distance to default, and of Bayesian parameter uncertainty .

7.1 THE FITTED FRAILTY MODEL

We now examine the fit of the frailty-based intensity model, estimated using the methods outlined in Chapter 6, to the data for matchable U.S. non-financial public firms described in Section 4.1. This section presents the basic results.

Table 7.1 shows the estimated covariate parameter vector $\widehat{v}$ and frailty parameters $\widehat{\eta}$ and $\widehat{\kappa}$ together with estimates of asymptotic standard errors. The signs, magnitudes, and statistical significance of the coefficients are similar to those without frailty reported in Chapter 4, with the exception of the coefficient for the 3-month Treasury bill rate, which is smaller without frailty. Using a Bayesian approach, Appendix E compares the qualities of fit of the models with and without frailty. The results suggest that the frailty-based model provides a substantially better fit.

Our results show important roles for both firm-specific and macroeconomic covariates. Distance to default, although a highly significant covariate, does not on its own determine the default intensity, but does explain a large part of the variation of default risk across companies and over time. For example a negative shock to distance to default by one standard deviation increases the default intensity by roughly $e^{1.2} - 1 \approx 230\%$. The one-year trailing stock return covariate proposed by Shumway (2001) has a highly significant impact on default intensities. Perhaps it is a proxy for firm-specific information that is not captured by distance to default. The coefficient linking the trailing S&P 500 return to a firm's default intensity is positive at conventional significance levels, and of the unexpected sign by univariate reasoning. Of course, with multiple covariates, the sign need not be evidence that a good year in the stock market is itself bad news for default risk. It could also be the case that, after boom years in the stock market, a firm's distance to default overstates its financial health.

Table 7.1: Maximum likelihood estimates of intensity-model parameters. The frailty volatility is the coefficient η of dependence of the default intensity on the OU frailty process Y. Estimated asymptotic standard errors are computed using the Hessian matrix of the expected complete data log likelihood at $\beta = \hat{\beta}$. The mean reversion and volatility parameters are based on monthly time intervals.

	Coefficient	Std. Error	t-statistic
constant	−1.029	0.201	−5.1
distance to default	−1.201	0.037	−32.4
trailing stock return	−0.646	0.076	−8.6
3-month T-bill rate	−0.255	0.033	−7.8
trailing S&P 500 return	1.556	0.300	5.2
latent-factor volatility η	0.125	0.017	7.4
latent-factor mean reversion κ	0.018	0.004	4.8

Source: Duffie, Eckner, Horel, and Saita (2009).

The estimate $\hat{\eta} = 0.125$ of the dependence of the unobservable default intensities on the frailty variable Y_t, corresponds to a monthly volatility of this frailty effect of 12.5%, which translates to an annual volatility of 43.3%, which is highly economically and statistically significant.

7.2 FILTERING THE FRAILTY PROCESS

The Gibbs sampler allows us to compute the $\mathcal{F}_T$-conditional posterior distribution of the frailty variable Y_t, where T is the final date of our sample. This is the conditional distribution of the latent factor given all of the historical default and covariate data through the end of the sample period. Figure 7.1 shows the conditional mean of the latent frailty factor, estimated as the average of 5,000 samples of Y_t drawn from the Gibbs sampler. One-standard-deviation bands are shown around the posterior mean. We see substantial fluctuations in the frailty effect over time. For example, the multiplicative effect of the expected frailty factor on default intensities in 2001 is roughly $e^{1.1}$, or approximately three times larger than during 1995. A comparison that is based on replacing $Y(t)$ in $E[e^{\eta Y(t)} \mid \mathcal{F}_t]$ with the posterior mean of $Y(t)$ works reasonably well because the Jensen effects associated with the expectations of $e^{\eta Y(t)}$ for times in 1995 and 2001 are roughly comparable.

Figure 7.1 suggests that the frailty factor was generally higher when defaults were more prevalent, during the recessions of 1989–1991 and 2001. In light of this, one might suspect mis-specification of the proportional-hazards intensity

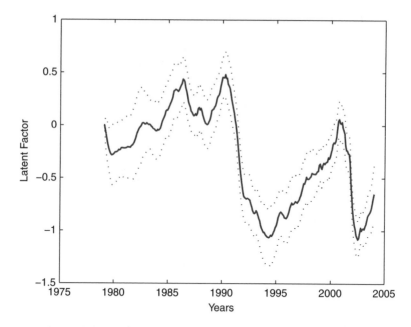

Fig. 7.1: Mean frailty path. Conditional posterior mean $E\,(\eta Y_t \mid \mathcal{F}_T)$ of the scaled latent Ornstein–Uhlenbeck frailty variable, with one-standard-deviation bands based on the $\mathcal{F}_T$-conditional variance of Y_t.

Source: Duffie, Eckner, Horel, and Saita (2009).

model (6.1), which would automatically induce a measured frailty effect if the true intensity model has a higher-than-proportional dependence on distance to default. If the response of the true log-intensity to variation in distance to default is convex, then the estimated latent variable in our current formulation would be higher when distances to default are well below normal, as in 1991 and 2003. Appendix G provides an extension of the model that incorporates non-parametric dependence of default intensities on distance to default. The results indicate that the proportional-hazards specification is unlikely to be a significant source of mis-specification in this regard. The response of the estimated log intensities is roughly linear in distance to default, and the estimated posterior of the frailty path has roughly the appearance shown in Figure 7.1.

Appendix F shows that our general conclusions regarding the role of the various covariates and frailty remain as stated after allowing for a significant degree of unobserved heterogeneity across firms.

Figure 7.1 illustrates the posterior distribution of the frailty variable Y_t given the information $\mathcal{F}_T$ available at the final time T of the sample period. Most

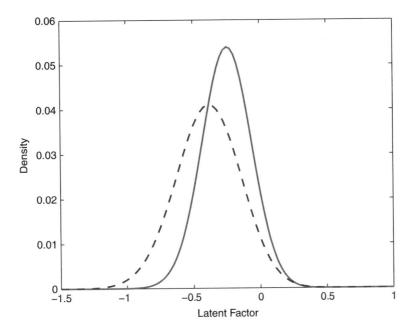

Fig. 7.2: Posterior frailty density. Conditional posterior density of the scaled frailty factor, ηY_t, for t in January 2000, given $\mathcal{F}_T$, that is, given all data (solid line), and given only contemporaneously available data in $\mathcal{F}_t$ (dashed line). These densities are calculated using the forward-backward recursions described in Section 7.2.

Source: Duffie, Eckner, Horel, and Saita (2009).

applications of a default-risk model would call for the posterior distribution of Y_t given only the current information $\mathcal{F}_t$. This is the relevant information for measurement by a bank of the risk of a portfolio of corporate debt.

Figure 7.2 compares the conditional density of Y_t for t at the end of January 2000, conditioning on $\mathcal{F}_T$ (in effect, the entire sample of default times and observable covariates up to 2004), with the density of Y_t when conditioning on only $\mathcal{F}_t$ (the data available up to and including January 2000). Given the additional information available at the end of 2004, the $\mathcal{F}_T$-conditional distribution of Y_t is more concentrated than that obtained by conditioning on only the concurrently available information, $\mathcal{F}_t$. The posterior mean of Y_t given the information available in January 2000 is lower than that given all of the data through 2004, reflecting the sharp rise in corporate defaults in 2001 above and beyond that predicted from the observed covariates alone.

Figure 7.3 shows the path over time of the contemporaneous conditional mean $E(\eta Y_t \mid \mathcal{F}_t)$ of the frailty process.

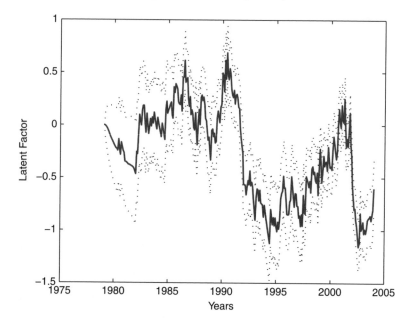

Fig. 7.3: Contemporaneous mean frailty path. Conditional mean $E(\eta Y_t \mid \mathcal{F}_t)$ and conditional one-standard-deviation bands of the scaled frailty variable, given only contemporaneously available data $(\mathcal{F}_t)$.

Source: Duffie, Eckner, Horel, and Saita (2009).

7.3 TERM-STRUCTURE OF DEFAULT RISK

We next examine the implications of frailty for the term structure of conditional default probabilities of a currently active firm i at time t, in terms of default hazard rates. As explained in Chapter 2, the conditional hazard rate is the conditional expected rate of default at time u, given both $\mathcal{F}_t$ and the event of survival up to time u.

As an illustration, we consider the term structure of default hazard rates of Xerox Corporation for three different models, *(i)* the basic model in which only observable covariates are considered, *(ii)* the model with the latent OU frailty variable, and *(iii)* the model with the common OU frailty variable as well as unobserved heterogeneity. Figure 7.4 shows the associated term structures of default hazard rates for Xerox Corporation in December 2003, given the available information at that time. The calculations shown account for the effect of other exits in the manner described in Chapter 3.

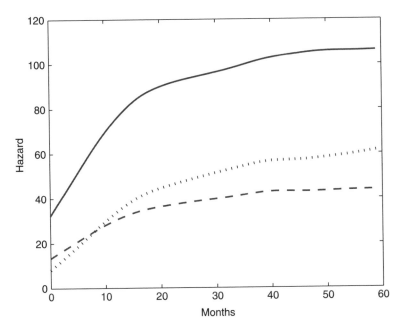

Fig. 7.4: Term structure of default risk for Xerox. The term structure of conditional hazard rates for Xerox Corporation in December 2003 for the model with frailty variable (solid line), the model without frailty variable (dashed line), and the model with frailty variable and unobserved heterogeneity (dotted line).

Source: Duffie, Eckner, Horel, and Saita (2009).

7.4 DEFAULT CORRELATION

As we have explained, in the model without frailty, firms' default times are correlated only as implied by the correlation of observable factors determining their default intensities. Without frailty, we found model-implied default correlations to be much lower than the sample default correlations estimated by deServigny and Renault (2002). The results of Chapter 5 confirm that the default correlations implied by the model without frailty are significantly understated. Common dependence on unobservable covariates, as in our model, allows a substantial additional channel of default correlation.

For a given conditioning date t and maturity date $u > t$, and for two given active firms i and j, the default correlation is the $\mathcal{F}_t$-conditional correlation between D_{iu} and D_{ju}, the default indicators for companies i and j, respectively. Figure 7.5 shows the effect of the latent frailty variable on the default correlation for two companies in our data set. We see that the latent factor induces additional correlation and that the effect is increasing as the time horizon increases.

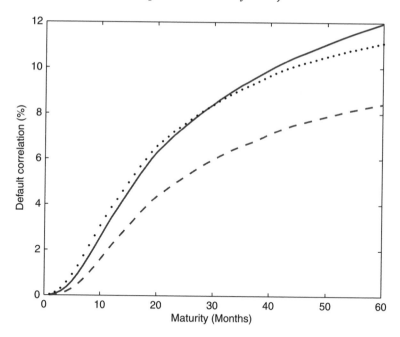

Fig. 7.5: Default correlation of Xerox and ICO. The term structure of correlation between the default indicators of ICO Incorporated and Xerox Corporation for the model with a common frailty (solid line), the model without a frailty (dashed line), and the model with frailty and unobserved heterogeneity (dotted line).

Source: Duffie, Eckner, Horel, and Saita (2009).

7.5 PORTFOLIO LOSS RISK

In our setting, allowing a common frailty variable increases the potential for defaults that are clustered in time. In order to illustrate the role of the common frailty effect in producing default clusters, we consider the distribution of the total number of defaults from a hypothetical portfolio consisting of all 1,813 companies in our data set that were active as of January 1998. We computed the posterior distribution, conditional on the information $\mathcal{F}_t$ available for t in January 1998, of the total number of defaults during the subsequent five years, January 1998 through December 2002. Figure 7.6 shows the probability density of the total number of defaults in this portfolio for three different models. All three models have the same posterior marginal distribution for each firm's default time, but the joint distribution of default times varies among the three models depending on how the common frailty process Y is substituted for each firm i with a firm-specific process Y_i that has the same posterior probability distribution as Y. Model (a) is the fitted model with a common frailty variable, that is, with $Y_i = Y$. For model (b), the initial condition Y_{it} of Y_i is common

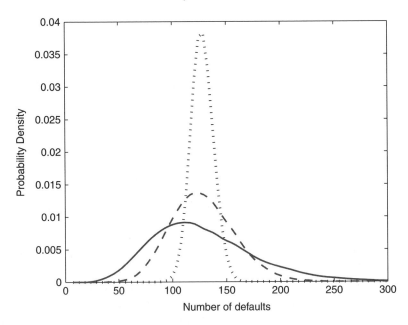

Fig. 7.6: Future portfolio default risk. The conditional probability density, given $\mathcal{F}_t$ for t in January 1998, of the total number of defaults within five years from the portfolio of all active firms at January 1998, in (a) the fitted model with frailty (solid line), (b) a hypothetical model in which the common frailty process Y is replaced with firm-by-firm frailty processes with initial condition at time t equal to that of Y_t, but with common Brownian motion driving frailty for all firms replaced with firm-by-firm independent Brownian motions (dashed line), and (c) a hypothetical model in which the common frailty process Y is replaced with firm-by-firm independent frailty processes having the same posterior probability distribution as Y (dotted line). The density estimates are obtained with a Gaussian kernel smoother (bandwidth equal to 5) applied to a Monte Carlo generated empirical distribution.

Source: Duffie, Eckner, Horel, and Saita (2009).

to all firms, but the future evolution of Y_i is determined not by the common OU-process Y, but rather by an OU-process Y_i that is independent across firms. Thus, Model (b) captures the default correlation associated with the current posterior distribution of Y_t, but has no common future frailty shocks. For Model (c), the hypothetical frailty processes of the firms, $Y_1, \ldots, Y_m$, are independent. That is, the initial condition Y_{it} is drawn independently across firms from the posterior distribution of Y_t, and the future shocks to Y_i are those of an OU-process Y_i that is independent across firms.

One can see that the impact of the frailty effect on the portfolio loss distribution is substantially affected both by uncertainty regarding the current level Y_t of common frailty in January 1998, and also by common future frailty shocks to different firms. Both of these sources of default correlation are above and beyond those associated with exposure of firms to observable macroeconomic shocks, and exposure of firms to correlated observable firm-specific shocks (especially correlated changes in leverage).

In particular, we see in Figure 7.6 that the two hypothetical models that do not have a common frailty variable assign virtually no probability to the event of more than 200 defaults between January 1998 and December 2002. The 95-percentile and 99-percentile losses of the model (c) with completely independent frailty variables are 144 and 150 defaults, respectively. Model (b), with independently evolving frailty variables with the same initial value in January 1998, has a 95-percentile and 99-percentile of 180 and 204 defaults, respectively. The actual number of defaults in our data set during this time period was 195.

The 95-percentile and 99-percentile of the loss distribution of the actual estimated model (a), with a common frailty variable, are 216 and 265 defaults, respectively. The realized number of defaults during this event horizon, 195, is slightly below the 91-percentile of the distribution implied by the fitted frailty model, therefore constituting a relatively extreme event. On the other hand, taking the hindsight bias into account, in that our analysis was partially motivated by the high number of defaults in the years 2001 and 2002, the occurrence of 195 defaults might be viewed from the perspective of the frailty-based model as only moderately severe.

7.6 OUT-OF-SAMPLE ACCURACY

In this section we examine the out-of-sample performance of the model with and without frailty.

We first review the out-of-sample ability of our model to sort firms according to estimated default likelihoods at various time horizons. Traditional tools for this purpose are the "power curve" and the associated "accuracy ratio." Given a future time horizon and a particular default prediction model, the power curve for out-of-sample default prediction is the function f that maps any x in $[0,1]$ to the fraction $f(x)$ of the firms that defaulted before the time horizon that were initially ranked by the model in the lowest fraction x of the population. For example, the 1-year power curve for the model estimated without frailty, illustrated in Figure 7.7, shows that the "worst" 20% of the firms in the sample, according to estimated 1-year default probabilities, accounted for approximately 92% of the firms that actually defaulted in the subsequent 1-year period, on average over the period 1993–2004. These results are out of sample, in that the model used to produce the estimated default probabilities is that estimated from data for 1980 to the end of 1992.

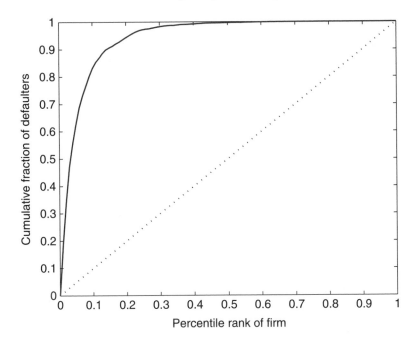

Fig. 7.7: Out-of-sample power curve. Average out-of-sample power curve for 1-year default prediction, January 1993 to December, 2003, for the model with no frailty effect. For each fraction x on the horizontal axis, the curve shows the fraction of the firms that defaulted within one year that were ranked in the lowest fraction x of firms according to estimated default probability at the beginning of the year, on average over the sample period.

Source: Duffie, Saita, and Wang (2007).

The accuracy ratio[1] associated with a given power curve is defined as twice the area between the power curve and the 45-degree line. So, a random-sort model has an expected accuracy ratio of approximately 0. A "crystal ball" (a perfect sort) has an accuracy ratio of 100% minus the ex post total fraction of firms that defaulted. The accuracy ratio is an industry benchmark for comparing the default prediction accuracy of different models.

Figure 7.8 shows 1-year accuracy ratios over the post-1993 sample periods for the intensity models estimated with and without the effect of frailty. These

---

[1] The "accuracy ratio" of a model with power curve f is defined as

$$2 \int_0^1 (f(x) - x)\, dx.$$

The identity, $x \mapsto r(x) = x$, is the expected power curve of a completely uninformative model, one that sorts firms randomly.

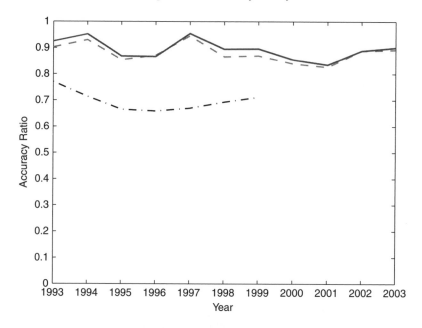

Fig. 7.8: Accuracy ratios. Out-of-sample accuracy ratios (ARs), based on models estimated with data up to December 1992. The solid line provides 1-year-ahead ARs based
on the model without frailty. The dashed line shows 1-year-ahead ARs for the model
with frailty. The dash-dot line shows 5-year-ahead ARs for the model with frailty.
Source: Duffie, Eckner, Horel, and Saita (2009).

accuracy ratios are essentially unchanged when replacing the model as estimated in 1993 with the sequence of models estimated at the beginnings of
each of the respective forecast periods. The 1-year-ahead out-of-sample average
accuracy ratio for default prediction from our model, over 1993–2003, is 88%.
The out-of-sample accuracy for prediction of merger and acquisition, however,
indicates no out-of-sample power to discriminate among firms regarding their
likelihood of being merged or acquired.

As discussed by Duffie, Saita, and Wang (2007), the accuracy ratios of our
model without frailty are an improvement on those of any other model in the
available literature. As one can see from Figure 7.8, however, the accuracy ratios
are essentially unaffected by allowing for frailty. This may be due to the fact that,
because of the dominant role of the distance-to-default covariate, firms generally tend to be ranked roughly in order of their distances to default, which of
course do not depend on the intensity model. Accuracy ratios measure ordinal
(ranking) quality, and do not otherwise capture the out-of-sample ability of a
model to estimate the magnitudes of default probabilities.

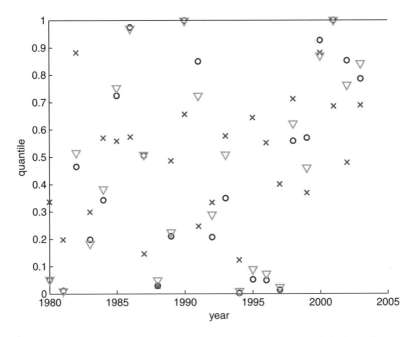

Fig. 7.9: Default quantiles. Quantiles of the realized number of defaults with respect to the predicted 1-year portfolio loss distribution as implied by the model with frailty (crosses) and without frailty variable (circles).

Source: Duffie, Eckner, Horel, and Saita (2009).

We next consider the out-of-sample behavior of total portfolio defaults for the models with and without frailty. Specifically, at the beginning of each year between 1980 and 2003, we calculate for the companies in our data set the model-implied distribution of the number of defaults during the subsequent 12 months, and then determine the quantile of the realized number of defaults with respect to this distribution. For a correct model, the quantiles are uniformly distributed on $[0, 1]$.

Figure 7.9 shows these quantiles for the models estimated with and without frailty. The quantiles of the model without frailty seem to cluster near 0 and 1, suggesting that the model without frailty tends to underestimate the probabilities of large or small numbers of defaults. For example, in 1994 the realized number of defaults lies below the 0.5-percentile of the predicted portfolio default distribution, while in 1990 and 2001 the realized number of defaults lies above the 99.9-percentile of predicted portfolio default distribution. On the other hand, the quantiles for the model with frailty are distributed more evenly in the unit interval, indicating a more accurate assessment of credit risk at the portfolio level.

The forecasting errors for the model without frailty tend to be serially correlated over time. This indication of mis-specification is most evident for the periods 1994–1997 as well as 2000–2003. The null hypothesis of no serial correlation in the quantiles is indeed rejected at the 1% significance level for the model without frailty. On the other hand, with a p-value of 0.64, the null hypothesis of no serial correlation in the quantiles cannot be rejected for the model with frailty.

7.7 CONCLUDING REMARKS

Our results indicate that, after controlling for a reasonable selection of observable covariates, U.S. corporates are exposed to a common unobserved source of default risk that increases default correlation and extreme portfolio loss risk above and beyond that implied by the observable common and correlated macroeconomic and firm-specific sources of default risk that were used to fit the model. We estimated a model of corporate default intensities in the presence of a time-varying latent frailty factor, and with unobserved heterogeneity. The previous chapter provided a method for fitting the model parameters using a combination of the Monte Carlo EM algorithm and the Gibbs sampler. This method also provides the conditional posterior distribution of the Ornstein–Uhlenbeck frailty process.

Applying this model to data for U.S. firms between January 1979 and March 2004, we find that corporate default rates vary over time well beyond levels that can be explained by a model that includes only our selection of observable covariates. In particular, the posterior distribution of the frailty variable shows that the expected rate of corporate defaults was much higher in 1989–1990 and 2001–2002, and much lower during the mid-1990s and in 2003–2004, than those implied by an analogous model without frailty. An out-of-sample test for data between 1980 and 2003 indicates that a model without frailty would significantly underestimate the probability of extremely high or low default losses in portfolios of corporate credits, while a model with frailty gives a more accurate assessment of credit risk on the portfolio level.

We estimate that the frailty variable represents a common unobservable factor in default intensities with an annual volatility of roughly 45%. The estimated rate of mean reversion of the frailty factor, 1.8% per month, implies that when defaults cluster in time to a degree that is above and beyond that suggested by observable default-risk factors, the half-life of the impact of this unobservable factor is roughly 3 years. Unfortunately, however, we find that the mean-reversion rate is difficult to pin down with the available data, as indicated by the Bayesian posterior density of the frailty mean-reversion parameter shown in Appendix H.

The relative importance of frailty will decline with improvements in the selection of covariates. Lando and Nielsen (2009) have already offered some guidance on this front. It nevertheless seems important to allow for the role of hidden or unobservable sources of default correlation in applications that call for estimates of the likelihood of large numbers of defaults.

Our methodology could be applied to other situations in which a common unobservable factor is suspected to play an important role in the time-variation of arrivals for certain events, for example mergers and acquisitions, mortgage prepayments and defaults, or leveraged buyouts.

APPENDIX A

Time-Series Parameter Estimates

This appendix provides the estimates from Duffie et al. (2007) of the time-series model of covariates that is specified in Chapter 4.

For the two-factor interest-rate parameters, our maximum likelihood parameter estimates, with standard errors in subscripted parentheses, are

$$k_r = \begin{pmatrix} 0.03_{(0.026)} & -0.021_{(0.030)} \\ -0.027_{(0.012)} & 0.034_{(0.014)} \end{pmatrix},$$

$$\theta_r = \begin{pmatrix} 3.59_{(4.08)} \\ 5.47_{(3.59)} \end{pmatrix},$$

and

$$C_r = \begin{pmatrix} 0.5639_{(0.035)} & 0 \\ 0.2247_{(0.026)} & 0.2821_{(0.008)} \end{pmatrix},$$

where θ_r is measured in percentage points.

Joint maximum likelihood estimation of equations (4.2), (4.3), and (4.4), simultaneously across all firms i in $\{1, \ldots, n\}$ gives the parameter estimates (with standard errors shown in subscripted parentheses):

$$b = \begin{pmatrix} 0.0090_{(0.0021)} & -0.0121_{(0.0024)} \end{pmatrix}'$$

$$k_D = 0.0355_{(0.0003)}$$

$$\sigma_D = 0.346_{(0.0008)}$$

$$k_v = 0.015_{(0.0002)}$$

$$\sigma_v = 0.1169_{(0.0002)}$$

$$AA' + BB' = \begin{pmatrix} 1 & 0.448_{(0.0023)} \\ 0.448_{(0.0023)} & 1 \end{pmatrix}$$

$$BB' = \begin{pmatrix} 0.0488_{(0.0038)} & 0.0338_{(0.0032)} \\ 0.0338_{(0.0032)} & 0.0417_{(0.0033)} \end{pmatrix}$$

$$k_S = 0.1137_{(0.018)}$$

$$\alpha_S = 0.047_{(0.0019)}$$

$$\theta_S = 0.1076_{(0.0085)}$$

$$\gamma_S = \begin{pmatrix} 0.0366_{(0.0032)} & 0.0134_{(0.0028)} \end{pmatrix}.'$$

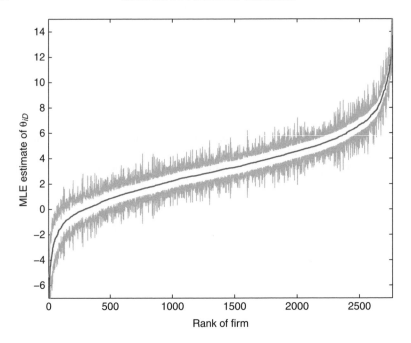

Fig. A.1: Cross-sectional distribution of estimated targeted distance to default. For each firm i, the maximum likelihood estimate $\hat{\theta}_{iD}$ of the target for distance to default is shown, along with the asymptotic estimate (plotted vertically) of a one-standard-deviation error band.

Source: Duffie, Saita, and Wang (2007).

Figure A.1 shows the cross-sectional distribution of estimated targeted distance to default, $\hat{\theta}_{iD}$, with standard errors.

Residual Gaussian Copula Correlation

Here, we will define the notion of a copula, provide a brief critique of the manner in which copula models have been applied in the financial industry, and describe the empirical fit of a "residual copula model" that estimates the extent to which the default correlation in our public-firm default data is not explained by the default intensities estimated in Chapter 4.

Consider default times $\tau_1, \ldots, \tau_n$ whose cumulative distribution functions (CDFs) $F_1, \ldots, F_n$ are, for simplicity, assumed to be strictly increasing and continuous. The copula for $\tau_1, \ldots, \tau_n$ is defined as the joint probability distribution of the (uniformly distributed) random variables $F_1(\tau_1), \ldots, F_n(\tau_n)$. If there are joint Gaussian variables $X_1, \ldots, X_n$ with CDFs $G_1, \ldots, G_n$ such that C is also the joint probability distribution of $G_1(X_1), \ldots, G_n(X_n)$, then we say that the copula of $\tau_1, \ldots, \tau_n$ is Gaussian. A Gaussian copula, although not necessarily realistic in default-time applications, is easy to apply. For example, the default times can be simulated with the copula-implied joint distribution by first simulating $X_1, \ldots, X_n$ and then letting $\tau_i = F_i^{-1}(G_i(X_i))$. In financial-industry practice, it has been common to address portfolio default risk with a Gaussian copula. In fact, for many practical applications, it is assumed that the default times $\tau_1, \ldots, \tau_n$ have the same CDFs, and moreover that the correlation of any pair of the underlying Gaussian variables is the same as the correlation of any other pair. The single correlation parameter is said to be the "flat Gaussian-copula correlation." This surprisingly simple copula is undoubtedly too simple for most default-risk applications.

Putting aside the disadvantages associated with the lack of realism of commonly used copula models, the copula approach to modeling correlated default times is hampered by the lack of any tractable accompanying framework for computing conditional default risk given information about the borrowers that can arrive over time, such as the market prices of credit default swaps. There is no role in the definition of the copula for auxiliary new information, beyond the information revealed by the arrival of the defaults themselves.

Salmon (2009) provides a popular account of the problems created by the dependence of the financial industry on the Gaussian copula model of correlated default risk, leading up to the financial crisis of 2007–2009.

Schönbucher and Schubert (2001) suggested a model that allows one to augment the effect of correlation induced through doubly-stochastic default intensity processes with additional correlation parameterized through a copula model. In order to gauge the degree to which default correlation in our data on U.S. public corporations is not captured by the default intensity processes estimated in Chapter 4, Das, Duffie, Kapadia, and Saita (2007) calibrated the intensity-conditional copula model of Schönbucher and Schubert (2001) to these intensity processes and the associated observed default times. Specifically, they estimated the amount of copula correlation that must be added, after conditioning on the intensities, to match the upper-quartile moments of the empirical distribution of defaults per time bin. This measure of residual default correlation depends on the specific copula model. Here, we employ the industry-standard flat (single-parameter) Gaussian copula. The resulting calibrated Gaussian copula correlation is a measure of the degree of correlation in default times that is not captured by co-movement in default intensities. This "residual" Gaussian copula correlation is estimated by the following algorithm.

1. We fix a particular correlation parameter r and cumulative-intensity bin size c.

2. For each name i and each bin number k, we calculate the increase in cumulative intensity $C_i^{c,k}$ for name i that occurs in this bin. (The intensity for this name stays at zero until name i appears, and the cumulative intensity stops growing after name i disappears, whether by default or otherwise.)

3. For each scenario j of 5,000 independent scenarios, we draw one of the bins, say k, at random (equally likely), and draw joint standard normal $X_1, \ldots, X_n$ with $\mathrm{corr}(X_i, X_m) = r$ whenever i and m differ.

4. For each i, we let $U_i = G(X_i)$, the standard normal cumulative distribution function $G(\cdot)$ evaluated at X_i, and draw "default" for name i in bin k if $U_i > \exp(-C_i^{c,k})$.

5. A correlation parameter r is "calibrated" to the data for bin size c, to the nearest 0.01, if the associated upper-quartile mean across simulated samples best approximates the upper-quartile mean of the actual data reported in Table 5.3.

The results are reported in Table B.1. As anticipated by the tests reported in Chapter 5, the calibrated residual Gaussian copula correlation r is non-negative for all time bins, and ranges from 0.01 to 0.04. The largest estimate is for bin size 10; the smallest is for bin size 2.

Table B.1: Residual Gaussian copula correlation. Using a Gaussian copula for intensity-conditional default times and equal pairwise correlation r for the underlying normal variables, Monte Carlo means are shown for the upper quartile of the empirical distribution of the number of defaults per bin. Set in boldface is the correlation parameter r at which the Monte Carlo estimated mean best approximates the empirical counterpart. (Under the null hypothesis of correctly measured intensities, the theoretical residual Gaussian copulation r is approximately zero.)

Bin size	Mean of upper copula correlation quartile (data)	Mean of simulated upper quartile copula correlation				
		$r = 0.00$	$r = 0.01$	$r = 0.02$	$r = 0.03$	$r = 0.04$
2	4.00	3.87	**4.01**	4.18	4.28	4.48
4	7.39	6.42	6.82	7.15	**7.35**	7.61
6	9.96	8.84	9.30	9.74	**10.13**	10.55
8	12.27	11.05	11.73	**12.29**	12.85	13.37
10	16.08	13.14	14.01	14.79	15.38	**16.05**

Source: Das, Duffie, Kapadia, and Saita (2007).

We can place these "residual" copula correlation estimates in perspective by referring to Akhavein, Kocagil, and Neugebauer (2005), who estimate an unconditional Gaussian copula correlation parameter of approximately 19.7% within sectors and 14.4% across sectors by calibrating with empirical default correlations (that is, before "removing," as we do, the correlation associated with covariance in default intensities).[1] Although only a rough comparison, this indicates that correlation of default intensities accounts for a large fraction, but not all of the default correlation.

[1] Their estimate is based on a method suggested by deServigny and Renault (2002). Akhavein, Kocagil, and Neugebauer (2005) provide related estimates.

APPENDIX C

Additional Tests for Mis-Specified Intensities

This appendix reports the results of additional tests of the default intensities estimated in Chapter 4.

C.1 Testing for Independent Increments

Although the tests reported in Chapter 5 depend to some extent on the independent-increments property of Poisson processes, we now test specifically for serial correlation of the numbers of defaults in successive time bins. That is, under the null hypothesis of correctly estimated intensities, and fixing an accumulative total default intensity of c per time bin, the numbers of defaults $N_1, N_2, \ldots, N_K$ in successive bins are independent and identically distributed. We test for independence by estimating the autoregressive model

$$N_k = A + BN_{k-1} + \epsilon_k, \tag{C.1}$$

Table C.1: Excess default autocorrelation. Estimates of the autoregressive model (C.1) of excess defaults in successive bins, for a range of bin sizes (t-statistics are shown parenthetically). Under the hypothesis of correctly measured default intensities, fixing an accumulative total default intensity of c per time bin, the numbers of defaults $N_1, N_2, \ldots, N_K$ in successive bins are independent and identically distributed. The parameters A and B are the intercept and autoregression coefficient, respectively, in (C.1).

Bin size	No. of Bins	$A(t_A)$	$B(t_B)$	R^2
2	230	2.091	0.019	0.0004
		(0.506)	(0.286)	
4	116	2.961	0.304	0.0947
		(−2.430)	(3.438)	
6	77	4.705	0.260	0.0713
		(−1.689)	(2.384)	
8	58	5.634	0.338	0.1195
		(−2.090)	(2.733)	
10	46	7.183	0.329	0.1161
		(−1.810)	(2.376)	

Source: Das, Duffie, Kapadia, and Saita (2007).

for coefficients A and B and for *iid* innovations $\epsilon_1, \epsilon_2, \ldots$ Under the joint hypothesis of correctly specified default intensities and the doubly stochastic property, $A = c$, $B = 0$, and $\epsilon_1, \epsilon_2 \ldots$ are *iid* demeaned Poisson random variables. A significantly positive estimate for the autoregressive coefficient B would be evidence against the null hypothesis. This could reflect missing covariates, whether they are unobservable (frailty) or are observable but missing from the estimated intensity model. For example, if a business-cycle covariate should be included but is not, and if this missing covariate is persistent across time, then defaults per bin would be fatter-tailed than the Poisson distribution, and there would be positive serial correlation in defaults per bin.

Table C.1 presents the results of this autocorrelation analysis. The estimated autoregressive coefficient B is mildly significant for bin sizes of 4 and larger (with t-statistics ranging from 2.37 to 3.43).

C.2 Missing Macroeconomic Covariates

Prior work by Lo (1986), Lennox (1999), McDonald and Van de Gucht (1999), Duffie, Saita, and Wang (2007), and Couderc and Renault (2004) suggests that macroeconomic performance is an important explanatory variable in default prediction. We now explore the potential role of missing macroeconomic default covariates. In particular, we examine *(i)* whether the inclusion of U.S. gross domestic product (GDP) or industrial production (IP) growth rates helps explain default arrivals after controlling for the default covariates that are already used to estimate our default intensities, and if so, *(ii)* whether the absence of these covariates could potentially explain the model test rejections reported in Chapter 5. We find that industrial production offers some explanatory power, but GDP growth rates do not.

Under the null hypothesis of no mis-specification, fixing a bin size of c, the number of defaults in a bin in excess of the mean, $Y_k = N_k - c$, is the increment of a martingale and therefore should be uncorrelated with any variable in the information set available prior to the formation of the k-th bin. Consider the regression

$$Y_k = \alpha + \beta_1 GDP_k + \beta_2 IP_k + \epsilon_k, \tag{C.2}$$

where GDP_k and IP_k are the growth rates of U.S. gross domestic product and industrial production observed in the quarter and month, respectively, that ends immediately prior to the beginning of the k-th bin. In theory, under the null hypothesis of correct specification of the default intensities, the coefficients α, β_1, and β_2 are zero. Table C.2 reports estimated regression results for a range of bin sizes.

We report the results for the multiple regression as well as for GDP and IP separately. For all bin sizes, GDP growth is not statistically significant, and is unlikely to be a candidate for explaining the residual correlation of defaults. Industrial production enters the regression with sufficient significance to warrant its consideration as an additional explanatory variable in the default intensity model. For each of the bins, the sign of the estimated IP coefficient is negative. That is, significantly more than the number of defaults predicted by the intensity model occur when industrial production growth rates are lower than normal, as anticipated by business-cycle reasoning, after controlling for other covariates.

Table C.2: Macroeconomic variables and default intensities. For each bin size c, ordinary least squares coefficients are reported for the regression of the number of defaults in excess of the mean, $Y_k = N_k - c$, on the previous quarter's GDP growth rate (annualized), and the previous month's growth in (seasonally adjusted) industrial production (IP). The number of observations is the number of bins of size c. Standard errors are corrected for heteroskedasticity; t-statistics are reported in parentheses. The GDP growth rates are annualized; the IP growth rates are not annualized.

Bin Size	No. Bins	Intercept	GDP	IP	R^2 (%)
2	230	0.28	−7.19		1.06
		(1.59)	(−1.43)		
		0.15		−41.96	1.93
		(1.21)		(−2.21)	
		0.27	−4.57	−35.70	2.31
		(0.17)	(−0.83)	(−1.68)	
4	116	0.46	−10.61		1.14
		(1.11)	(−0.91)		
		0.40		−109.28	5.49
		(1.60)		(−2.88)	
		0.53	−5.08	−103.27	5.73
		(1.41)	(−0.50)	(−2.51)	
6	77	1.12	−30.72		4.99
		(1.84)	(−2.12)		
		0.41		−155.09	7.55
		(−1.00)		(−1.89)	
		0.91	−18.09	−124.09	8.98
		(1.58)	(−1.18)	(−1.42)	
8	58	0.80	−19.64		1.81
		(0.85)	(−0.74)		
		1.35		−357.23	18.63
		(2.40)		(−3.65)	
		1.35	−0.08	−357.20	18.63
		(1.77)	(−0.00)	(−3.47)	
10	46	1.81	−49.00		5.89
		(1.57)	(−1.62)		
		0.45		−231.26	7.66
		(0.59)		(−2.07)	
		1.96	−41.45	−205.15	11.78
		(1.80)	(−1.38)	(−2.08)	

Source: Das, Duffie, Kapadia, and Saita (2007).

It is also useful to examine the role of missing macroeconomic factors when defaults are much higher than expected. Table C.3 provides the results of a test of whether the excess upper-quartile number of defaults (the mean of the upper quartile less the mean of the upper quartile for the Poisson distribution of parameter c, as examined previously in Table 5.3) are correlated with GDP and IP growth rates. We report two sets of regressions; the first set is based on the prior period's macroeconomic

Table C.3: Upper-tail regressions. For each bin size c, ordinary least squares coefficients are shown for the regression of the number of defaults observed in the upper quartile less the mean of the upper quartile of the theoretical distribution (with Poisson parameter equal to the bin size) on the previous and current GDP and industrial production (IP) growth rates. The number of observations is the number K of bins. Standard errors are corrected for heteroskedasticity; t-statistics are reported in parentheses.

Bin size	K	Intercept	Previous Qtr GDP	Previous month IP	$R^2(\%)$
2	77	0.28	1.40		0.00
		(1.55)	(0.22)		
		0.36		−57.75	4.92
		(2.08)		(−2.46)	
		0.16	8.99	−76.80	6.94
		(1.04)	(1.04)	(−2.11)	
4	48	0.41	−6.19		0.97
		(1.24)	(−0.71)		
		0.29		−65.83	3.88
		(−1.26)		(−1.64)	
		0.29	−22.15	−65.26	3.88
		(0.79)	(−0.02)	(−1.14)	

Bin size	K	Intercept	Current bin GDP	Current bin IP	$R^2(\%)$
2	77	0.45	−5.98		1.03
		(1.67)	(−0.82)		
		0.38		−47.20	2.82
		(2.04)		(−2.07)	
		0.36	0.98	−50.28	2.84
		(1.23)	(0.10)	(−1.56)	
4	48	0.83	−23.29		12.67
		(1.60)	(−2.44)		
		0.48		−77.93	17.88
		(1.90)		(−3.07)	
		0.63	−7.85	−62.55	18.63
		(1.78)	(−0.74)	(−2.30)	

Source: Das, Duffie, Kapadia, and Saita (2007).

variables, and the second set is based on the growth rates observed within the bin period.[1]

We report results for those bin sizes, 2 and 4, for which we have a reasonable number of observations. Once again, we find some evidence that industrial production growth rates help explain default rates, even after controlling for estimated intensities.

---

[1] The within-period growth rates are computed by compounding over the daily growth rates that are consistent with the reported quarterly growth rates.

In light of the possibility that U.S. industrial production growth (IP) is a missing covariate, we re-estimated default intensities after augmenting the list of covariates with IP. Indeed, IP shows up as a mildly significant covariate, with a coefficient that is approximately 2.2 times its standard error. (The original four covariates in (4.5) have greater significance, in this sense.) Using the estimated default intensities associated with this extended specification, we repeat all of the tests reported earlier.

Our primary conclusions remain unchanged. Albeit with slightly higher p-values, the results of all tests reported in Chapter 5 are consistent with those reported for the original intensity specification (4.5), and lead to a rejection of the estimated intensity model. For example, the goodness-of-fit test rejects the Poisson assumption for every bin size; the upper-tail tests analogous to those of Table 5.3 result in a rejection of the null at the 5% level for three of the five bins, and at the 10% level for the other two. The Prahl test statistic using the extended specification is 3.25 standard deviations from its null mean (as compared with 3.48 for the original model). The calibrated residual Gaussian copula correlation parameter r is the same for each bin size as that reported in Table B.1. Overall, even with the augmented intensity specification, the tests suggest more clustering than implied by correlated changes in the modeled intensities.

In more recent work, Lando and Nielsen (2009) have shown that substantial improvement in the intensity model estimated in Chapter 4 can be obtained by adding certain accounting ratios as additional covariates.

APPENDIX D

Applying the Gibbs Sampler with Frailty

In the setting of the frailty-correlated default model of Chapter 6, a central quantity of interest for describing and estimating the historical default dynamics is the posterior density $p_Y(\cdot \mid W, D, \beta)$ of the latent frailty process Y. This is a complicated high-dimensional density. It is prohibitively computationally intensive to directly generate samples from this distribution. Nevertheless, Markov Chain Monte Carlo (MCMC) methods can be used for exploring this posterior distribution by generating a Markov Chain over Y, denoted $\{Y^{(n)}\}_{n \geq 1}^N$, whose equilibrium path joint density is $p_Y(\cdot \mid W, D, \beta)$. Samples from the joint posterior distribution can then be used for parameter inference and for analyzing the properties of the frailty process Y. For a function $f(\cdot)$ satisfying regularity conditions, a Monte Carlo estimate of

$$E[f(Y) \mid W, D, \beta] = \int f(y) p_Y(y \mid W, D, \beta) \, dy \tag{D.1}$$

is given by

$$\frac{1}{N} \sum_{n=1}^{N} f\left(Y^{(n)}\right). \tag{D.2}$$

Under conditions, the ergodic theorem for Markov chains guarantees the convergence of this average to its expectation as $N \to \infty$. One such function of interest is the identity, $f(y) = y$, so that

$$E[f(Y) \mid W, D, \beta] = E[Y \mid W, D, \beta] = \{E(Y_t \mid \mathcal{F}_T) : 0 \leq t \leq T\},$$

the posterior mean of the path of the latent Ornstein–Uhlenbeck frailty process.

The linchpin to MCMC is that the joint distribution of the frailty path $Y = \{Y_t : 0 \leq t \leq T\}$ can be broken down into a set of conditional distributions. A general version of the Clifford–Hammersley (CH) Theorem (Hammersley and Clifford (1970) and Besag (1974)) provides conditions under which a set of conditional distributions characterizes a unique joint distribution. For example, in our setting, the CH Theorem implies that the density $p_Y(\cdot \mid W, D, \beta)$ of $\{Y_0, Y_1, \ldots, Y_T\}$ is uniquely determined by the following set of conditional distributions,

$$Y_0 \mid Y_1, Y_2, \ldots, Y_T, W, D, \beta$$
$$Y_1 \mid Y_0, Y_2, \ldots, Y_T, W, D, \beta$$
$$\vdots$$
$$Y_T \mid Y_0, Y_1, \ldots, Y_{T-1}, W, D, \beta,$$

using the naturally suggested interpretation of this informal notation. We refer the interested reader to Robert and Casella (2005) for an extensive treatment of Monte Carlo methods, as well as Johannes and Polson (2009) for an overview of MCMC methods applied to problems in financial economics.

In our case, the conditional distribution of Y_t at a single point in time t, given all of the observable variables (W, D) and given $Y_{(-t)} = \{Y_s : s \neq t\}$, is somewhat tractable, as shown below. This allows us to use the Gibbs sampler (Geman and Geman 1984; Gelman, Carlin, Stern, and Rubin 2004) to draw whole sample paths from the posterior distribution of $\{Y_t : 0 \leq t \leq T\}$ by the algorithm:

0. Initialize $Y_t = 0$ for $t = 0, \ldots, T$.

1. For $t = 1, 2, \ldots, T$, draw a new value of Y_t from its conditional distribution given $Y_{(-t)}$. For a method, see below.

2. Store the sample path $\{Y_t : 0 \leq t \leq T\}$ and return to Step 1 until the desired number of paths has been simulated.

We usually discard the first several hundred paths as a "burn-in" sample, because initially the Gibbs sampler has not approximately converged[1] to the posterior distribution of $\{Y_t : 0 \leq t \leq T\}$.

It remains to show how to sample Y_t from its conditional distribution given $Y_{(-t)}$. Recall that $\mathcal{L}(\beta \mid W, Y, D)$ denotes the complete-information likelihood of the observed covariates and defaults, where $\beta = (\nu, \eta, \kappa)$. For $0 < t < T$, we have

$$p\left(Y_t \mid W, D, Y_{(-t)}, \beta\right) = \frac{p(W, D, Y, \beta)}{p(W, D, Y_{(-t)}, \beta)}$$

$$\propto p(W, D, Y, \beta)$$

$$= p(W, D \mid Y, \beta) p(Y, \beta)$$

$$\propto \mathcal{L}(\beta \mid W, Y, D) \, p(Y, \beta)$$

$$= \mathcal{L}(\beta \mid W, Y, D) \, p(Y_t \mid Y_{(-t)}, \beta) p\left(Y_{(-t)}, \beta\right)$$

$$\propto \mathcal{L}(\beta \mid W, Y, D) \, p(Y_t \mid Y_{(-t)}, \beta),$$

where we repeatedly made use of the fact that terms not involving Y_t are constant.

From the Markov property it follows that the conditional distribution of Y_t given $Y_{(-t)}$ and β is the same as the conditional distribution of Y_t given Y_{t-1}, Y_{t+1} and β. Therefore

---

[1] We used various convergence diagnostics, such as trace plots of a given parameter as a function of the number of samples drawn, to assure that the iterations have proceeded long enough for approximate convergence and to assure that our results do not depend markedly on the starting values of the Gibbs sampler. See Gelman, Carlin, Stern, and Rubin (2004), Chapter 11.6, for a discussion of various methods for assessing convergence of MCMC methods. Conversations with Jun Liu and Xiao-Li Meng suggest caution regarding reliance on even moderately large burn-in samples.

$$p\left(Y_t \mid Y_{(-t)}, \beta\right) = p\left(Y_t \mid Y_{t-1}, Y_{t+1}, \beta\right)$$

$$= \frac{p\left(Y_{t-1}, Y_t, Y_{t+1} \mid \beta\right)}{p\left(Y_{t-1}, Y_{t+1} \mid \beta\right)}$$

$$\propto p\left(Y_{t-1}, Y_t, Y_{t+1} \mid \beta\right)$$

$$= p\left(Y_{t-1}, Y_t \mid \beta\right) p\left(Y_{t+1} \mid Y_{t-1}, Y_t, \beta\right)$$

$$\propto \frac{p\left(Y_{t-1}, Y_t \mid \beta\right)}{p\left(Y_{t-1} \mid \beta\right)} p\left(Y_{t+1} \mid Y_t, \beta\right)$$

$$= p\left(Y_t \mid Y_{t-1}, \beta\right) p\left(Y_{t+1} \mid Y_t, \beta\right),$$

where $p\left(Y_t \mid Y_{t-1}, \beta\right)$ is the one-step transition density of the OU-process (6.6). Hence,

$$p\left(Y_t \mid W, D, Y_{(-t)}, \beta\right) \propto \mathcal{L}\left(\beta \mid W, Y, D\right) \cdot p\left(Y_t \mid Y_{t-1}, \beta\right) p\left(Y_{t+1} \mid Y_t, \beta\right). \quad \text{(D.3)}$$

Equation (D.3) determines the desired conditional density of Y_t given Y_{t-1} and Y_{t+1} in an implicit form. Although it is not possible to directly draw samples from this distribution, we can employ the Random Walk Metropolis–Hastings algorithm (Metropolis and Ulam 1949; Hastings 1970).[2] We use the proposal density $q(Y_t^{(n)} \mid W, D, Y^{(n-1)}, \beta) = \phi_{0,4}(Y_t^{(n-1)})$, where ϕ_{μ,σ^2} denotes the Gaussian density with mean μ and variance σ^2. That is, we take the mean to be the value of Y_t from the previous iteration of the Gibbs sampler, and the variance to be twice the variance of the increments of the standard Brownian motion.[3] The Metropolis–Hastings step to sample Y_t in the *n-th* iteration of the Gibbs sampler therefore works as follows:

1. Draw a candidate $y \sim \phi_{0,4}(Y_t^{(n-1)})$.
2. Compute

$$\alpha\left(y, Y_t^{(n)}\right) = \min\left(\frac{\mathcal{L}\left(\beta \mid W, Y_{(-t)}^{(n-1)}, Y_t = y, D\right)}{\mathcal{L}\left(\beta \mid W, Y^{(n-1)}, D\right)}, 1\right). \quad \text{(D.4)}$$

3. Draw U with the uniform distribution on $(0, 1)$ and let

$$Y_t^{(n)} = \begin{cases} y & \text{if } U < \alpha\left(y, Y_t^{(n)}\right) \\ Y_t^{(n-1)} & \text{otherwise.} \end{cases}$$

[2] Alternatively, we could discretize the sample space and approximate the conditional distribution by a discrete distribution, an approach commonly referred to as the Griddy Gibbs method (Tanner (1998)). The Metropolis–Hastings algorithm is typically faster for cases in which the conditional density is not known explicitly.

[3] We calculated the conditional density for various points in time numerically to check for excessively fat tails, and found that using a normal proposal density does not appear to jeopardize the convergence of the Metropolis–Hastings algorithm. See Mengersen and Tweedie (1996) for technical conditions.

The choice of the acceptance probability (D.4) ensures that the Markov chain $\{Y_t^{(n)} : n \geq 1\}$ satisfies the detailed balance equation

$$p\left(y_1 | W, D, Y_{(-t)}, \beta\right) \phi_{y_1,4}\left(y_2\right) \alpha\left(y_1, y_2\right) = p\left(y_2 | W, D, Y_{(-t)}, \beta\right) \phi_{y_2,4}\left(y_1\right) \alpha\left(y_2, y_1\right).$$

Moreover, $\{Y_t^{(n)} : n \geq 1\}$ has $p\left(Y_t | W, D, Y_{(-t)}, \beta\right)$ as its stationary distribution. (For this, see for example Theorem 7.2 of Robert and Casella (2005).)

APPENDIX E

Testing for Frailty

In order to judge the relative fit of the models of Chapters 3 and 6, that is, without frailty and with frailty, we do not use standard tests, such as the χ^2 test. Instead, we compare the marginal likelihoods of the models. This approach does not rely on large-sample distribution theory and has the intuitive interpretation of attaching prior probabilities to the competing models.

Specifically, we consider a Bayesian approach to comparing the quality of fit of competing models and assume positive prior probabilities for the two models "noF" (the model without frailty) and "F"(the model with a common frailty variable). The posterior odds ratio is

$$\frac{\mathbb{P}(F \mid W, D)}{\mathbb{P}(noF \mid W, D)} = \frac{\mathcal{L}_F(\widehat{\gamma}_F, \widehat{\beta}_F \mid W, D)}{\mathcal{L}_{noF}(\widehat{\gamma}_{noF}, \widehat{\beta}_{noF} \mid W, D)} \frac{\mathbb{P}(F)}{\mathbb{P}(noF)}, \tag{E.1}$$

where $\widehat{\beta}_M$ and $\mathcal{L}_M$ denote the maximum likelihood estimator and the likelihood function for a given model M, respectively. Substituting (6.5) into (E.1) leaves

$$\frac{\mathbb{P}(F \mid W, D)}{\mathbb{P}(noF \mid W, D)} = \frac{\mathcal{L}(\widehat{\gamma}_F \mid W) \, \mathcal{L}_F(\widehat{\beta}_F \mid W, D)}{\mathcal{L}(\widehat{\gamma}_{noF} \mid W) \, \mathcal{L}_{noF}(\widehat{\beta}_{noF} \mid W, D)} \frac{\mathbb{P}(F)}{\mathbb{P}(noF)}$$

$$= \frac{\mathcal{L}_F(\widehat{\beta}_F \mid W, D)}{\mathcal{L}_{noF}(\widehat{\beta}_{noF} \mid W, D)} \frac{\mathbb{P}(F)}{\mathbb{P}(noF)}, \tag{E.2}$$

using the fact that the time-series model for the covariate process W is the same in both models. The first factor on the right-hand side of (E.2) is sometimes known as the "Bayes factor."

Following Kass and Raftery (1995) and Eraker et al. (2003), we focus on the size of the statistic Φ given by twice the natural logarithm of the Bayes factor, which is on the same scale as the likelihood ratio test statistic. An outcome of Φ between 2 and 6 provides positive evidence, an outcome between 6 and 10 provides strong evidence, and an outcome larger than 10 is very strong evidence for the alternative model. This criterion does not necessarily favor more complex models due to the marginal nature of the likelihood functions in (E.2). See Smith and Spiegelhalter (1980) for a discussion of the penalizing nature of the Bayes factor, sometimes referred to as the "fully automatic Occam's razor." In our case, the outcome of the test statistic is 22.6. In the sense of this approach to model comparison, we see relatively strong evidence in favor of including a frailty variable. Unfortunately, the Bayes factor cannot be used for comparing the model with frailty to the model with frailty and unobserved heterogeneity, since for the latter model evaluating the likelihood function is computationally prohibitively expensive.

Unobserved Heterogeneity

The Monte Carlo EM algorithm described in Section 6.2 and the Gibbs sampler described in Appendix D are extended here to treat unobserved heterogeneity. We describe in this appendix the extended algorithm and estimates.

The corresponding extension of the Monte Carlo EM algorithm is:

0. Initialize $Z_i^{(0)} = 1$ for $1 \leq i \leq m$ and initialize $\beta^{(0)} = (\hat{v}, 0.05, 0)$, where $\hat{v}$ is the maximum likelihood estimator of v in the model without frailty.

1. (Monte Carlo E-step.) Given the current parameter estimate $\beta^{(k)}$, draw samples $(Y^{(j)}, Z^{(j)})$ for $j = 1, \ldots, n$ from the joint posterior distribution $p_{Y,Z}(\cdot \mid W, D, \beta^{(k)})$ of the frailty sample path $Y = \{Y_t : 0 \leq t \leq T\}$ and the vector $Z = (Z_i : 1 \leq i \leq m)$ of unobserved heterogeneity variables. This can be done, for example, by using the Gibbs sampler described below. The expected complete-data log likelihood is now given by

$$Q\left(\beta, \beta^{(k)}\right) = E_{\beta^{(k)}}\left(\log \mathcal{L}\left(\beta \mid W, Y, Z, D\right)\right)$$

$$= \int \log \mathcal{L}\left(\beta \mid W, y, z, D\right) p_{Y,Z}\left(y, z \mid W, D, \beta^{(k)}\right) dy \, dz. \qquad \text{(F.1)}$$

Using n sample paths generated by the Gibbs sampler, (F.1) can be approximated by

$$\widehat{Q}\left(\beta, \beta^{(k)}\right) = \frac{1}{n} \sum_{j=1}^{n} \log \mathcal{L}\left(\beta \mid W, Y^{(j)}, Z^{(j)}, D\right). \qquad \text{(F.2)}$$

2. (M-step.) Maximize $\widehat{Q}(\beta, \beta^{(k)})$ with respect to the parameter vector β, using the Newton–Raphson algorithm. Set the new parameter estimate $\beta^{(k+1)}$ equal to this maximizing value.

3. Replace k with $k + 1$, and return to Step 2, repeating the MC E-step and the M-step until reasonable numerical convergence.

The Gibbs sampler for drawing from the joint posterior distribution of $\{Y_t : 0 \leq t \leq T\}$ and $\{Z_i : 1 \leq i \leq m\}$ works as follows:

0. Initialize $Y_t = 0$ for $t = 0, \ldots, T$. Initialize $Z_i = 1$ for $i = 1, \ldots, m$.

1. For $t = 1, \ldots, T$ draw a new value of Y_t from its conditional distribution given Y_{t-1}, Y_{t+1} and the current values for Z_i. This can be done using a straightforward modification of the Metropolis–Hastings algorithm described in Appendix D by treating $\log Z_i$ as an additional covariate with corresponding coefficient in (6.1) equal to 1.

2. For $i = 1, \ldots, m$, draw the unobserved heterogeneity variables $Z_1, \ldots, Z_m$ from their conditional distributions given the current path of Y. See below.

3. Store the sample path $\{Y_t, 0 \le t \le T\}$ and the variables $\{Z_i : 1 \le i \le m\}$. Return to Step 1 and repeat until the desired number of scenarios has been drawn, discarding the first several hundred as a burn-in sample.

It remains to show how to draw the heterogeneity variables $Z_1, \ldots, Z_m$ from their conditional posterior distribution. First, we note that

$$p(Z \mid W, Y, D, \beta) = \prod_{i=1}^{m} p(Z_i \mid W_i, Y, D_i, \beta),$$

by the conditional independence of the unobserved heterogeneity variables $Z_1, Z_2, \ldots, Z_m$. In order to draw Z from its conditional distribution, it therefore suffices to show how to draw each Z_i from its conditional distribution. Recall that we have specified the heterogeneity variable Z_i to be gamma distributed with mean 1 and standard deviation 0.5. A short calculation shows that, in this case, the density parameters a and b are both 4. Applying Bayes' rule,

$$p(Z_i \mid W, Y, D, \beta) \propto p_\Gamma(Z_i; 4, 4) \, \mathcal{L}(\beta \mid W_i, Y, Z_i, D_i)$$

$$\propto Z_i^3 e^{-4Z_i} e^{-\sum_{t=t_i}^{T_i} \lambda_{it} \Delta t} \prod_{t=t_i}^{T_i} [D_{it} \lambda_{it} \Delta t + (1 - D_{it})], \tag{F.3}$$

where $p_\Gamma(\,\cdot\,; a, b)$ is the density of a gamma distribution with parameters a and b. Substituting (6.7) into (F.3) gives

$$p(Z_i \mid W, Y, D, \beta) \propto Z_i^3 e^{-4Z_i} \exp\left(-\sum_{t=t_i}^{T_i} \tilde{\lambda}_{it} e^{\gamma Y_t} Z_i\right) \prod_{t=t_i}^{T_i} [D_{it} \lambda_{it} \Delta t + (1 - D_{it})]$$

$$= Z_i^3 e^{-4Z_i} \exp(-A_i Z_i) \cdot \begin{cases} B_i Z_i & \text{if company } i \text{ did default} \\ 1 & \text{if company } i \text{ did not default} \end{cases}, \tag{F.4}$$

Table F.1: Parameter estimates with frailty and unobserved heterogeneity. Maximum likelihood estimates of the intensity parameters in the model with frailty and unobserved heterogeneity. Asymptotic standard errors are computed using the Hessian matrix of the likelihood function at $\beta = \widehat{\beta}$.

	Coefficient	Std. error	t-statistic
constant	−0.895	0.134	−6.7
distance to default	−1.662	0.047	−35.0
trailing stock return	−0.427	0.074	−5.8
3-month T-bill rate	−0.241	0.027	−9.0
trailing S&P 500 return	1.507	0.309	4.9
latent factor volatility	0.112	0.022	5.0
latent factor mean reversion	0.061	0.017	3.5

Source: Duffie et al. (2009).

for company-specific constants A_i and B_i. The factors in (F.4) can be combined to give

$$p\left(Z_i \mid W_i, Y, D_i, \beta\right) = p_\Gamma\left(Z_i; 4 + D_{i,T_i}, 4 + A_i\right). \qquad \text{(F.5)}$$

This is again a gamma distribution, but with different parameters, and it is therefore easy to draw samples of Z_i from its conditional distribution.

Table F.1 shows the maximum likelihood estimates of the coeffcient ν_i associated with each observable covariate, the frailty parameters η and κ, and their estimated standard errors. We see that, while including unobserved heterogeneity decreases the coefficient η of dependence (sometimes interpreted as volatility) of the default intensity on the OU frailty process Y from 0.125 to 0.112, our general conclusions regarding the economic significance of the covariates and the importance of including a frailty process remain unaltered. We have also verified that that the estimated posterior distribution of the frailty process Y is qualitatively similar to that without allowing for unobserved heterogeneity.

APPENDIX G

Non-Linearity Check

So far, as specified by (6.1), we have assumed a linear dependence of the logarithm of the default intensity on the covariates. This assumption might be overly restrictive, especially in the case of the distance to default, which explains most of the variation of default intensities across companies and across time. If the response of the true log-intensity to distance to default is convex, then the latent frailty variable in our current formulation would be higher when distances to default go well below normal and *vice versa*. Such a mis-specification could be a potential source of the estimated posterior mean of the frailty path shown in Figure 7.1.

To check the robustness of our findings with respect to this log-linearity assumption, we therefore re-estimate the model using a non-parametric model for the contribution of distance to default. This model replaces the distance-to-default covariate

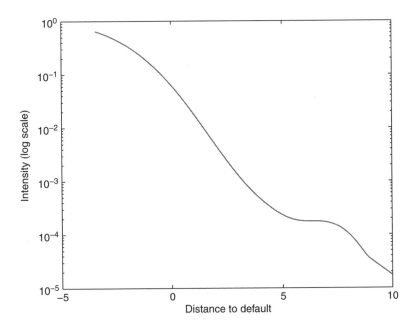

Fig. G.1: Non-parametric estimate of the dependence of annual default frequency on the current level of distance to default. For values of distance to default less than 9, a Gaussian kernel smoother with bandwidth of 1 was used to obtain the intensity estimate. For distances to default larger than 9, a log-linear relationship was assumed.

Source: Duffie, Eckner, Horel, and Saita (2009).

Table G.1: Frailty parameter estimates with non-parametric control for distance to default. Maximum likelihood estimates of the intensity parameters β in the model with frailty, replacing distance to default with $-\log(f(\delta))$, where $\delta(t)$ is distance to default and $f(\cdot)$ is the non-parametric kernel estimated mapping from δ to annual default frequency, illustrated in Figure G.1. The frailty volatility is the coefficient η of dependence of the default intensity on the standard Ornstein–Uhlenbeck frailty process Y. Estimated asymptotic standard errors were computed using the Hessian matrix of the expected complete data log-likelihood at $\beta = \widehat{\beta}$.

	Coefficient	Std. Error	t-statistic
Constant	2.279	0.194	11.8
$-\log(f(\delta))$	−1.198	0.042	−28.6
Trailing stock return	−0.618	0.075	−8.3
3-month T-bill rate	−0.238	0.030	−8.1
Trailing S&P 500 return	1.577	0.312	5.1
Latent factor volatility	0.128	0.020	6.3
Latent factor mean reversion	0.043	0.009	4.8

Source: Duffie, Eckner, Horel, and Saita (2009).

with $-\log f(\delta(t))$, where $\delta(t)$ is the distance to default and $f(x)$ is the non-parametric kernel-smoothed fit of 1-year frequency of default in our sample at a distance to default of x. Figure G.1 shows the kernel-smoothed non-parametric relationship between the current level of distance to default, $\delta(t)$, and the annualized default intensity. For values of $\delta(t) \leq 9$, a Gaussian kernel smoother with bandwidth equal to one was used to obtain the intensity estimate, whereas due to lack of data the tail of the distribution was approximated by a log-linear relationship, smoothly extending the graph in Figure 4.1.

Using this extension, we re-estimated the model parameters. Table G.1 shows the estimated covariate parameter vector $\widehat{\nu}$ and frailty parameters $\widehat{\eta}$ and $\widehat{\kappa}$, together with asymptotic estimates of standard errors.

Comparing Tables 7.1 and G.1, we see no noteworthy changes in the estimated coefficients linking a firm's covariates to its default intensity. In particular, the coefficient now linking the default intensity and $-\log f(\delta(t))$ is virtually the same as the coefficient for $\delta(t)$ in the original model. The intercept coefficient estimate has changed from −1.20 to 2.28 largely due to the fact that $-\log f(\delta(t)) \approx \delta(t) - 3.5$. Indeed, for the intercept at $\delta(t) = 0$ in Figure G.1, we have $10^{-1.5} \approx 0.032 \approx \exp(-1.20 - 2.28)$. We have checked that the posterior path of the latent Ornstein–Uhlenbeck frailty process seems essentially unchanged.

APPENDIX H

Bayesian Frailty Dynamics

The analysis of default risk provided in Chapters 6 and 7 is based in part on maximum likelihood estimation of the frailty mean-reversion and volatility parameters, κ and σ. Uncertainty regarding these parameters could lead to an increase in the tail risk of portfolio losses, which we investigate in this appendix.

The stationary variance of the frailty process Y is

$$\sigma_\infty^2 \equiv \lim_{s \to \infty} \text{var}\,(Y_s \mid \mathcal{G}_t) = \lim_{s \to \infty} \text{var}\,(Y_s \mid Y_t) = \frac{\sigma^2}{2\kappa}.$$

Motivated by the historical behavior of the posterior mean of the frailty, we take the prior density of the stationary standard deviation, σ_∞, to be gamma distributed with a mean of 0.5 and a standard deviation of 0.25. The prior distribution for the mean-reversion rate κ is also assumed to be gamma, with a mean of $\log 2/36$ (which corresponds to a half-life of three years for shocks to the frailty variable) and a standard deviation of $\log 2/72$. The joint prior density of σ and κ is therefore of the form

$$p\,(\sigma, \kappa) \propto \left(\frac{\sigma}{\sqrt{2\kappa}} \right)^3 \exp\left(-\frac{8\sigma}{\sqrt{2\kappa}} \right) \kappa^3 \exp\left(-\kappa \frac{144}{\log 2} \right).$$

Figure H.1 shows the marginal posterior densities of the volatility and mean reversion parameters of the frailty process, conditional on the data. Figure H.2 shows their joint

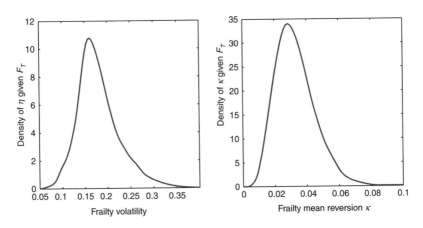

Fig. H.1: Bayesian parameters for frailty dynamics. Marginal posterior densities, given $\mathcal{F}_T$, of the frailty volatility parameter η and the frailty mean reversion rate κ in the Bayesian approach of this appendix.

Source: Duffie, Eckner, Horel, and Saita (2009).

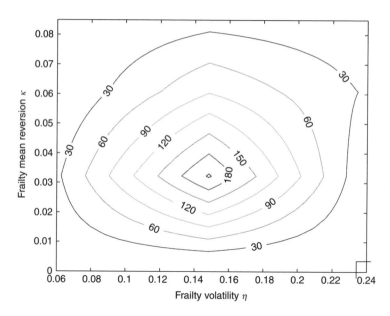

Fig. H.2: Bayesian joint distribution of frailty dynamic parameters. Isocurves of the joint posterior density, given $\mathcal{F}_T$, of the frailty volatility parameter η and mean reversion rate κ.

Source: Duffie, Eckner, Horel, and Saita (2009).

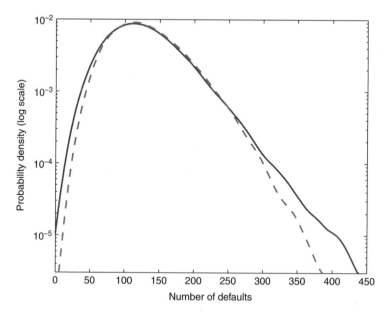

Fig. H.3: Bayesian versus non-Bayesian portfolio risk. Density, on a logarithmic scale, of the number of defaults in the portfolio treated by Figure 7.6, when fixing the volatility and mean reversion parameter at their MLE estimates as in Figure 7.6 (dashed line), and in the Bayesian estimation framework (solid line). The density estimates were obtained by applying a Gaussian kernel smoother (with a bandwidth of 10) to the Monte Carlo generated empirical distribution.

Source: Duffie, Eckner, Horel, and Saita (2009).

posterior density. These figures indicate considerable posterior uncertainty regarding these dynamic parameters. From the viewpoint of subjective probability, estimates of the tail risk of the portfolio loss distribution that are obtained by fixing these common frailty parameters at their maximum likelihood estimates might significantly underestimate the probability of extreme portfolio losses.

Although parameter uncertainty has a minor influence on portfolio loss distribution at intermediate quantiles, Figure H.3 reveals a moderate impact of parameter uncertainty on the extreme tails of the probability distribution of portfolio defaults that was estimated in Chapter 7 without Bayesian parameter uncertainty. For example, when fixing the frailty parameters η and κ at their maximum likelihood estimates, the 99-percentile of the distribution is 265 firm defaults. Taking posterior parameter uncertainty into account, this quantile rises to 275 defaults.

Risk-Neutral Default Probabilities

This appendix introduces a change of probability measure that allows the pricing of risk for default timing to be captured by distortions of the "true" default probabilities. This typically leads to a substantial upward adjustment of default intensities, as shown by Berndt, Douglas, Duffie, and Ferguson (2005).

Fixing a probability space $(\Omega, \mathcal{F}, P)$ and an information filtration $\{\mathcal{G}_t : t \geq 0\}$ satisfying the usual conditions,[1] we consider a stopping time τ with an intensity process λ, as defined in Chapter 2.

We suppose that a short-term interest rate process[2] r allows an investment of one unit of account at any time s to generate a total market value of $e^{\int_s^t r(u)\,du}$ at any time $t > s$. As defined by Harrison and Kreps (1979), an equivalent martingale measure is a probability measure P^*, whose events of positive probability are the same as those of P, with the property that any financial security paying Z at[3] a stopping time T has a market value at any time $t < T$ of

$$E^* \left(e^{-\int_t^T r(s)\,ds} Z \mid \mathcal{G}_t \right),$$

where E^* denotes expectation with respect to P^*. There can be many equivalent martingale measures. We proceed by fixing one of these, say P^*. As shown in finite-dimensional settings by Harrison and Kreps (1979), the existence of an equivalent martingale measure is essentially equivalent to the absence of arbitrage, meaning, roughly speaking, the absence of trading strategies requiring no investment and generating positive profits with probability one.

Proposition 4 (Artzner and Delbaen (1995)) *Suppose that P^* is a probability measure equivalent to P and T is a stopping time. Then T has an intensity under P if and only if T has an intensity under P^*.*

Under a given equivalent martingale measure P^*, we will call the intensity λ^* of a stopping time T the "risk-neutral intensity" of T. We will often wish to exploit a change of measure under which the doubly-stochastic property is preserved. A sufficient condition on the risk-premium process λ^*/λ is implied by Proposition 6, Appendix I, of Duffie (2001).

For cases in which the doubly stochastic property fails under P^*, ruling out the convenient risk-neutral survival probability calculation

$$P^*(\tau > t) = E^* \left(e^{-\int_0^t \lambda(s)\,ds} \right),$$

---

[1] See Protter (2004) for technical definitions.

[2] The process r is progressively measurable with respect to $\{\mathcal{G}_t : t \geq 0\}$, with $\int_0^t |r(s)|\,ds < \infty$ for all t.

[3] Here, Z is $\mathcal{G}_T$-measurable with $E^* \left(e^{-\int_t^T r(s)\,ds} |Z| \right) < \infty$.

Collin-Dufresne, Goldstein, and Huggonier (2004) provide a further change of probability measure, mentioned in Chapter 2, under which we can use a similar calculation.

Default risk pricing premia go beyond those arising from a distinction between the actual and risk-neutral intensities, λ and λ^*. We could have $\lambda_t^* = \lambda_t$ for all t, but obtain risk premia from a difference between the probability distributions of λ under the actual and equivalent martingale measures P and P^*. Sufficient conditions for this pricing setting are given by Jarrow, Lando, and Yu (2005). Specifically, suppose that T is doubly stochastic under P and P^* with the same intensity $\lambda = \lambda^*$ under these measures. Even in this case, we could have lower risk-neutral than actual survival probabilities whenever

$$P^*(T > t) = E^* \left(e^{-\int_0^t \lambda^*(s)\, ds} \right)$$

$$= E^* \left(e^{-\int_0^t \lambda(s)\, ds} \right)$$

$$< E \left(e^{-\int_0^t \lambda(s)\, ds} \right)$$

$$= P(\tau > t),$$

for example because $E^*(\lambda_t) > E(\lambda_t)$ for $t > 0$ due to dependence of the default intensity on risk factors whose expected future paths are more adverse to survival under the risk-neutral probability measure P^* than under the actual probability measure P. In general, there are two channels for default risk premia: *(i)* differences between the outcomes of actual and risk-neutral default intensities, and *(ii)* differences between the actual and risk-neutral probability distributions of risk factors that affect default intensities.

Bibliography

Akhavein, J. D., A. E. Kocagil, and M. Neugebauer (2005). A Comparative Empirical Study of Asset Correlations. Working Paper, Fitch Ratings, New York.

Allen, L. and A. Saunders (2003). A Survey of Cyclical Effects in Credit Risk Measurement Models. BIS Working Paper 126, Basel Switzerland.

Altman, E. I. (1968). Financial Ratios, Discriminant Analysis, and the Prediction of Corporate Bankruptcy. *Journal of Finance 23*, 589–609.

Andersen, P. K., O. Borgan, R. D. Gill, and N. Keiding (1992). *Statistical Models Based on Counting Processes*. New York: Springer-Verlag.

Artzner, P. and F. Delbaen (1995). Default Risk and Incomplete Insurance Markets. *Mathematical Finance 5*, 187–195.

Azizpour, S., K. Giesecke, G. Schwenkler (2010). Exploring the Sources of Default Clustering. Working Paper, Stanford University.

Baum, L. E., T. P. Petrie, G. Soules, and N. Weiss (1970). A Maximization Technique Occurring in the Statistical Analysis of Probabilistic Functions of Markov Chains. *Annals of Mathematical Statistics 41*, 164–171.

Beaver, B. (1968 Autumn). Market Prices, Financial Ratios, and the Prediction of Failure. *Journal of Accounting Research*, 170–192.

Berndt, A., R. Douglas, D. Duffie, and M. Ferguson (2005). Measuring Default-Risk Premia from Default Swap Rates and EDFs. Working Paper, Carnegie-Mellon University.

Besag, J. (1974). Spatial Interaction and The Statistical Analysis Of Lattice Systems. *Journal of the Royal Statistical Association: Series B 36*, 192–236.

Bharath, S. and T. Shumway (2008). Forecasting Default with the Merton Distance-to-Default Model. *Review of Financial Studies 21*, 1339–1369.

Black, F. and M. Scholes (1973). The Pricing of Options and Corporate Liabilities. *Journal of Political Economy 81*, 637–654.

Blume, M. and D. Keim (1991). Realized Returns and Volatility of Low-Grade Bonds: 1977–1989. *Journal of Finance 46*, 49–74.

Cappé, O., E. Moulines, and T. Rydén (2005). *Inference in Hidden Markov Models*. New York: Springer Verlag.

Celeux, G. and J. Diebolt (1986). The SEM Algorithm: A Probabilistic Teacher Algorithm Derived from the EM Algorith For The Mixture Problem. *Computational Statistics Quaterly 2*, 73–82.

Chava, S. and R. Jarrow (2004). Bankruptcy Prediction with Industry Effects. *Review of Finance 8*, 537–569.

Cochran, W. (1954). Some Methods of Strengthening χ^2 Tests. *Biometrics 10*, 417–451.

Collin-Dufresne, P., R. Goldstein, and J. Helwege (2010). Is Credit Event Risk Priced? Modeling Contagion via the Updating of Beliefs. Working Paper, Columbia University.

Collin-Dufresne, P., R. Goldstein, and J. Huggonier (2004). A General Formula for Valuing Defaultable Securities. *Econometrica 72*, 1377–1407.

Couderc, F. and O. Renault (2004). Times-to-Default: Life Cycle, Global and Industry Cycle Impacts. Working Paper, University of Geneva.

Crosbie, P. J. and J. R. Bohn (2002). Modeling Default Risk. Technical Report, KMV, LLC.

Das, S., D. Duffie, N. Kapadia, and L. Saita (2007). Common Failings: How Corporate Defaults are Correlated. *Journal of Finance 62*, 93–117.

Davis, M. and V. Lo (2001). Infectitious Default. *Quantitative Finance 1*, 382–387.

Delloy, M., J.-D. Fermanian, and M. Sbai (2005). Estimation of a Reduced-Form Credit Portfolio Model and Extensions to Dynamic Frailties. Working Paper, BNP-Paribas.

Demptser, A. P., N. M. Laird, and D. B. Rubin (1977). Maximum Likelihood Estimation from Incomplete Data via the EM Algorithm (with Discussion). *Journal of the Royal Statistical Society: Series B 39*, 1–38.

deServigny, A. and O. Renault (2002). Default Correlation: Empirical Evidence. Working Paper, Standard and Poors.

Duffie, D. (2001). *Dynamic Asset Pricing Theory* (3rd, Edition). Princeton, New Jersey: Princeton University Press.

Duffie, D., A. Eckner, G. Horel, and L. Saita (2009). Frailty Correlated Default. *Journal of Finance 64*, 2089–2123.

Duffie, D. and D. Lando (2001). Term Structures of Credit Spreads with Incomplete Accounting Information. *Econometrica 69*, 633–664.

Duffie, D., J. Pan, and K. Singleton (2000). Transform Analysis and Asset Pricing for Affine Jump-Diffusions. *Econometrica 68*, 1343–1376.

Duffie, D., L. Saita, and K. Wang (2007). Multi-Period Corporate Default Prediction with Stochastic Covariates. *Journal of Financial Economics 83*, 635–665.

Eckner, A. (2009). Computational Techniques for Basic Affine Models of Portfolio Credit Risk. *Journal of Computational Finance 13*, 63–97.

Eraker, B., M. Johannes, and N. Polson (2003). The Impact of Jumps in Volatility and Returns. *Journal of Finance 58*, 1269–1300.

Fisher, E., R. Heinkel, and J. Zechner (1989). Dynamic Capital Structure Choice: Theory and Tests. *Journal of Finance 44*, 19–40.

Fons, J. (1991). An Approach to Forecasting Default Rates. Working Paper, Moody's Investors Services.

Gelman, A., J. B. Carlin, H. S. Stern, and D. B. Rubin (2004). *Bayesian Data Analysis, 2nd Edition*. New York: Chapman and Hall.

Geman, S. and D. Geman (1984). Stochastic Relaxation, Gibbs Distributions, and the Bayesian Restoration of Images. *IEEE Transactions on Pattern Analysis and Machine Intelligence 6*, 721–741.

Giesecke, K. (2004). Correlated Default with Incomplete Information. *Journal of Banking and Finance 28*, 1521–1545.

Gordy, M. (2003). A Risk-Factor Model Foundation for Ratings-Based Capital Rules. *Journal of Financial Intermediation 12*, 199–232.

Hammersley, J. and P. Clifford (1970). Markov Fields on Finite Graphs and Lattices. Working Paper, Oxford University.

Harrison, M. and D. Kreps (1979). Martingales and Arbitrage in Multiperiod Security Markets. *Journal of Economic Theory 20*, 381–408.

Hastings, W. K. (1970). Monte-Carlo Sampling Methods using Markov Chains and Their Applications. *Biometrika 57*, 97–109.

Hillegeist, S. A., E. K. Keating, D. P. Cram, and K. G. Lundstedt (2004). Assessing the Probability of Bankruptcy. *Review of Accounting Studies 9*, 5–34.

Jacobsen, M. (2006). *Point Process Theory and Applications: Marked Point and Piecewise Deterministic Processes*. Boston, Birkhäuser.

Jarrow, R., D. Lando, and F. Yu (2005). Default Risk and Diversification: Theory and Applications. *Mathematical Finance 15*, 1–26.

Jarrow, R. and F. Yu (2001). Counterparty Risk and the Pricing of Defaultable Securities. *Journal of Finance 56*, 1765–1800.

Johannes, M. and N. Polson (2009). MCMC Methods For Continuous-Time Financial Econometrics. In Y. Ait-Sahalia and L. Hansen (Eds.), *Handbook of Financial Econometrics, Volume 2 Applications*, Chapter 1, pp. 1–72. Amsterdam: Elsevier.

Jonsson, J. and M. Fridson (1996, June). Forecasting Default Rates on High-Yield Bonds. *The Journal of Fixed Income*, 69–77.

Jorion, P. and G. Zhang (2007). Good and Bad Credit Contagion: Evidence from Credit Default Swaps. *Journal of Financial Economics 84*, 860–883.

Kass, R. and A. Raftery (1995). Bayes Factors. *Journal of The American Statistical Association 90*, 773–795.

Kavvathas, D. (2001). Estimating Credit Rating Transition Probabilities for Corporate Bonds. Working Paper, University of Chicago.

Kealhofer, S. (2003, January–February). Quantifying Credit Risk I: Default Prediction. *Financial Analysts Journal*, 30–44.

Koopman, S., A. Lucas, and A. Monteiro (2008). The Multi-State Latent Factor Intensity Model for Credit Rating Transitions. *Journal of Econometrics 142*, 399–424.

Koopman, S., A. Lucas, and B. Schwaab (2010). Macro, Frailty, and Contagion Effects in Defaults: Lessons from the 2008 Credit Crisis. Working Paper, University of Amsterdam.

Kusuoka, S. (1999). A Remark on Default Risk Models. *Advances in Mathematical Economics 1*, 69–82.

Lando, D. and M. S. Nielsen (2009). Correlation in Corporate Defaults: Contagion or Conditional Independence? Working Paper, University of Copenhagen.

Lando, D. and T. Skødeberg (2002). Analyzing Rating Transitions and Rating Drift with Continuous Observations. *Journal of Banking and Finance 26*, 423–444.

Lane, W. R., S. W. Looney, and J. W. Wansley (1986). An Application of the Cox Proportional Hazards Model to Bank Failure. *Journal of Banking and Finance 10*, 511–531.

Lang, L. and R. Stulz (1992). Contagion and Competitive Intra-Industry Effects of Bankruptcy Announcements. *Journal of Financial Economics 32*, 45–60.

Lee, S. H. and J. L. Urrutia (1996). Analysis and Prediction of Insolvency in the Property-Liability Insurance Industry: A Comparison of Logit and Hazard Models. *The Journal of Risk and Insurance 63*, 121–130.

Leland, H. (1994). Corporate Debt Value, Bond Covenants, and Optimal Capital Structure. *Journal of Finance 49*, 1213–1252.

Lennox, C. (1999). Identifying Failing Companies: A Reevaluation of the Logit, Probit, and DA Approaches. *Journal of Economics and Business 51*, 347–364.

Lo, A. (1986). Logit versus Discriminant Analysis: Specification Test and Application to Corporate Bankruptcies. *Journal of Econometrics 31*, 151–178.

McDonald, C. G. and L. M. Van de Gucht (1999). High-Yield Bond Default and Call Risks. *Review of Economics and Statistics 81*, 409–419.

Mengersen, K. and R. L. Tweedie (1996). Rates of Convergence of the Hastings and Metropolis Algorithms. *Annals of Statistics 24*, 101–121.

Merton, R. C. (1974). On the Pricing of Corporate Debt: The Risk Structure of Interest Rates. *Journal of Finance 29*, 449–470.

Metropolis, N. and S. Ulam (1949). The Monte Carlo Method. *Journal of The American Statistical Association 44*, 335–341.

Meyer, P.-A. (1971). Représentation Intégrale des Fonctions Excessives. Résultats de Mokobodzki. In P.-A. Meyer (Ed.), *Séminaire de Probabilités V*, Volume 191 of *Lecture Notes in Mathematics*, Berlin: Springer, pp. 196–208.

Nielsen, S. F. (2000). The Stochastic EM Algorithm: Estimation and Asymptotic Results. *Bernoulli 6*, 457–489.

Pickles, A. and R. Crouchery (1995). A Comparison of Frailty Models for Multivariate Survival Data. *Statistics in Medicine 14*, 1447–1461.

Prahl, J. (1999). A Fast Unbinned Test on Event Clustering in Poisson Processes. Working Paper, University of Hamburg.

Protter, P. (2004). *Stochastic Integration and Differential Equations, 2nd Edition*. New York: Springer-Verlag.

Rabiner, L. R. (1989). A Tutorial on Hidden Markov Models and Selected Applications in Speech Recognition. *Proceedings of the IEEE 77*, 257–285.

Robert, C. and G. Casella (2005). *Monte Carlo Statistical Methods*, (2nd Edition). New York: Springer Verlag.

Salmon, F. (2009). Recipe for Disaster: The Formula that Killed Wall Street. *Wired Magazine*, February 23, 2009.

Schönbucher, P. (2003). Information Driven Default Contagion. Working Paper, Eidgenössische Technische Hochschule, Zurich.

Schönbucher, P. and D. Schubert (2001). Copula Dependent Default Risk in Intensity Models. Working Paper, Bonn University.

Shumway, T. (2001). Forecasting Bankruptcy More Accurately: A Simple Hazard Model. *Journal of Business 74*, 101–124.

Smith, A. F. M. and D. J. Spiegelhalter (1980). Bayes Factors and Choice Criteria For Linear Models. *Journal of the Royal Statistical Society: Series B 42*, 213–220.

Tanner, M. A. (1998). *Tools for Statistical Inference: Methods for the Exploration of Posterior Distributions and Likelihood Functions, 3rd Edition*. New York: Springer-Verlag.

Vasicek, O. (2004). Probability of Loss on Loan Portfolio. In P. Carr (Ed.), *Derivatives Pricing*, Chapter 9. London: Risk Books.

Vassalou, M. and Y. Xing (2004). Default Risk in Equity Returns. *Journal of Finance 59*, 831–868.

Wei, G. C. and M. A. Tanner (1990). A Monte Carlo Implementation of the EM Algorithm and The Poor Man's Data Augmentation Algorithm. *Journal of The American Statistical Association 85*, 699–704.

Wu, C. F. J. (1983). On the Convergence Properties of the EM Algorithm. *Annals of Statistics 11*, 95–103.

Yu, F. (2003). Default Correlation in Reduced Form Models. *Journal of Investment Management 3*, 33–42.

Yu, F. (2005). Accounting Transparency and the Term Structure of Credit Spreads. *Journal of Financial Economics 75*, 53–84.

Zhang, Z. (2009). Recovery Rates and Macroeconomic Conditions: The Role of Loan Covenants. Working Paper, Boston College.

Zhou, C. (2001). An Analysis of Default Correlation and Multiple Defaults. *Review of Financial Studies 14*, 555–576.

Index

Note: Page numbers followed by "*f*" and "*t*" refer to figures and tables, respectively.

CA ROSE

THE CORSICAN
MOB BOOK 1

A. HAYAT

CAGED ROSE

ALSO BY A. HAYAT

Vows of a Mobster series
Mafia Bride series
Cocaine Hustler series
The Corsican Mob series
Cruel King series

Never miss a release, and follow the author on
Instagram @agkbooks

Notices

This is not a standalone novel and is intended to unfold over a few volumes. It ends in a cliffhanger.

This is a dark depiction of the world of organized crime and mafia, not for the faint of heart.

This story contains mature themes, sexual situations, strong language, graphic violence and explores sensitive topics which some readers may find upsetting or triggering. Reader discretion is advised. Intended for adults 18+ only.

Please do not read this series if you are easily offended. The opinions expressed by the characters in no way reflect the opinions of the author.

If you relate to any of the topics discussed, such as domestic abuse, mental health, blackmail, extortion or assault, please remember that you are not alone. Speak to somebody, or call the Samaritans, Childline, the police and so on.

Any alternating point of views are made clear with the chapter title names.

BLURB

When I saw her from across the bar with her pretty little face, her big brown eyes, her long brown hair and her beautiful, fuck-me body, I just knew that I would never be able to shake her from my damn mind. She turned my life upside down from the day I fucking laid eyes on her.

But then, the situation changed. She saw something she shouldn't have seen. Found out who I really was. The truth behind my rugged exterior.

But you know the rules of the Corsican Mafia. No witnesses…

So I had to take her in. I had to make her my hostage. And I had to make her my wife…

Whether she liked it or not.

PROLOGUE
ROSE

I could feel my lungs constrict as I watched the situation play itself out to me.

Feeling like the walls were closing in on me.

Feeling like I was suffocating…

And I couldn't breathe.

I couldn't fucking breathe.

My eyes fogged with tears, as my whole life flashed before my eyes.

Watching the assassin pull the fucking trigger, and my husband fall backwards onto the floor.

So much blood…

So much fucking blood.

I let out a terrified, blood-curdling scream as I leapt towards my husband and took him into my arms, trembling the entire time, hardly able to keep myself upright, as my surroundings continued to spin around me.

"You had it fucking coming to you, you bastard," the assassin gritted.

He turned to his other men.

"Let's go boys. *Deja que este hijo de puta sangre.*"

Let this motherfucker bleed.

I wept as I cradled Alejandro against my chest, just wishing that he wouldn't give up on me.

Wishing that he wouldn't stop fighting.

That he'd do his best to stay alive…

For me…

For *us*.

This couldn't be the end…

Not by a long shot.

We'd been through too much together for our love story to just end now.

"Please, Alejandro…" I wept against him, my tears mangling with his blood.

I screamed bloody murder as I kissed his mouth, and then began pumping his chest desperately.

Desperately trying to keep the oxygen flowing inside of him.

But it was no use…

He grew weaker and weaker against my grip, his cries getting quieter with every passing second.

Tick tock, tick tock…

Tick tock, tick *tock*.

"Alejandro, you can't leave me," I wept, clasping his face in my hands, wishing that his eyes would stay open.

"It's okay R – Rose…" he quivered shakily. "It's time for me to g – go…"

"NO!" I screamed, convulsing. "No, Alejandro, please don't speak like this!"

"I've been a dead man walking for a l – long time, Rose," he breathed. "This is the price I have to pay… For the fucked-up life I lived."

"Don't you dare speak like this is your fault!" I bawled. "None of this is your fault, Alejandro! You couldn't have known that they were coming! You couldn't have known that any of this was going to happen!"

"L – let me die, R – Rose…" he trembled. "Please forgive me. For not putting you first, for n – not treating you as good as I should have treated you. There's so much I w – want to say…"

"Don't you dare speak like this, Alejandro," I wept. "This isn't the end. You're not leaving me. You're not leaving me…"

"I love you R – Rose. No matter what anybody says… Just know that I always 1 – loved you…"

And then his head lulled backwards as a blood-curdling scream leapt out of my mouth.

Wishing that it was me in his place.

Wishing that it didn't have to be like this.

Not knowing what I was going to do without him.

My love…

My life.

He took the last piece of my soul with him as he died.

1
ROSE

I let out a blood-curdling scream, as I jolted upwards from my sleep.

Sweating profusely, my vision hazy, as I spun back into consciousness.

And I realized that I wasn't back in that dark place I'd been in so many years ago...

Because I saw curtains on the wall, a window,

my warm bed.

I was at home.

I was *safe*.

I rubbed my eyes groggily, my heart thumping erratically against my chest, as I did my best to soothe my nerves.

I had yet another nightmare about the night my husband was murdered in cold blood.

The night my life was ripped apart.

The night my heart was battered into shreds.

Broken beyond repair.

It had been a long time since my husband was murdered.

For years, I would scream.

Scream and cry until I was blue in the face.

Until my throat went dry.

Until my voice box went hoarse.

Screaming until I couldn't scream anymore.

I did my best to avenge Alejandro's death.

To seek justice.

But the cops never found out who was behind it…

And no matter how hard I tried, no matter how much I dug, how much I tried to scorch the area, CCTV, possible witnesses…

It all lead to a dead trail.

A dead trail to nowhere.

And still, the nightmares wouldn't stop.

They wouldn't fucking stop…

No matter how hard I tried to move on.

No matter how hard I tried to forget about what happened.

No matter how hard I tried to bury my skeletons in the closet.

To shut off all the bad memories.

It was no use…

Because they would keep replaying themselves.

Over and over to me in my head, like a form of motherfucking torture.

As if it was punishment.

My punishment for what had happened.

For not finding out who was behind it.

I couldn't help but to feel like I'd failed Alejandro.

Failed our love…

Failed our relationship.

I'd tried my hardest, and I knew that no matter how much harder I tried…

I would get nowhere.

I needed to move forward.

I needed to bury this in the past for good…

To shut off the nightmares permanently.

And to do that…

I needed *closure*.

2
ROSE

My heart thumped against my chest, as I got up from bed, and made my way to the bathroom.

Taking my time to shower, exfoliate, brush my hair, and moisturize.

I made my way to my closet, picking out Alejandro's favourite outfit that he loved seeing me in.

A long, black, V-neck, backless maxi dress that enunciated my curves.

The dress I wore on our second anniversary.

I swiped my face with honey-coloured foundation and concealer, and put on some lipstick and jewellery.

And then I took a deep breath out…

As I stared at my reflection.

"My name is Rose Rodriguez. I'm thirty-five years old. I'm an accountant, living in Spain. I live alone, in solitude. And today…"

I swallowed down a lump in my throat.

"I'm going to say goodbye to my ex-husband."

3
ROSE

I dusted myself off, before making my way out
of my apartment. I dialled into my mobile
phone keypad to call a cab, sweating profusely
the entire time.

"Where to, Miss?" the cab driver asked, as he
pulled up to the curb.

I did my best to remain brave and strong, calm and collected, even though inside, my heart was in my throat the entire time.

"To the cemetery," I swallowed.

"You got it."

***

It wasn't long before the cab driver set off…

Picking up speed with each passing second.

Twenty miles per hour…

Thirty miles per hour…

Forty miles per hour…

I stared out of the window, as my thoughts began hounding me in my head.

Knowing that I needed to do this.

I couldn't keep living like this.

Hating myself…

Despising myself for what happened to Alejandro that night.

I needed to accept things for how they were.

I needed to move on.

I just hoped that Alejandro would have it in his heart to forgive me…

If he was out there, watching over me in heaven, watching over me in limbo…

Wherever he was.

4
ROSE

I stepped out of the cab, and it drove away.

Taking a deep breath in, and a deep breath out, a deep breath in, and a deep breath out...

I made my way to the grave of Alejandro Rodriguez.

I could feel my eyes well with tears as I knelt down next to his grave.

Looking up at the headstone, the flowers scattered around it.

The lettering on the tombstone read:

"Alejandro Rodriguez. Husband, worker, friend. Gone but never forgotten. Forever in our hearts."

Silent tears rolled down my cheeks, as my heart twisted into knots. I finally plucked up the courage to speak.

"Hi Alejandro," I swallowed, my fingers tracing against the lettering. "I miss you so much. There hasn't been a day that's gone where I haven't thought about you. You're all that's on my mind, every second, every hour. Even though it's been years since you left me, left this world. It doesn't change the way I felt about you."

I trailed off my sentence, heaving my chest.

"I've tried so hard to come to terms with what's happened. I've tried so hard to avenge your death. You would probably be rolling in your grave right now if you knew that I haven't gotten anywhere with it.

"I tried so hard, and I wish you could see how hard I've tried. How much I chased up the cops to keep pursuing the case. To keep going with it, despite how many times they tried to close it. How much I dug CCTV, articles, newspapers. How much I scorched. But I got nowhere. It always led to a dead trail. And it kills me that I couldn't find the thugs responsible for this.

"I've been beating myself up about this for so long. For so many years. Feeling responsible for your death. Punishing myself for not finding the culprits. Feeling like I've failed you. Feeling like I haven't brought you to justice. And I can't keep living like this. It's no life for me to live.

"It's got to the point that I can't even look at myself or recognise myself in the mirror anymore. It's got to the point that I despise myself, hate myself, blaming myself for everything that's happened in this fucked-up life I've lived. And honestly, Alejandro… It feels like I'm losing myself in the process.

"There's so much I want to say to you. And I'm going to lay out all my cards on the table now. Because in all honesty, this has been eating me alive. I don't know if you're out there, watching over me, whether you're in heaven, whether you're in limbo. If only you could see how much this has damaged me, how much my heart is broken beyond repair.

"I need to move on, Alejandro. And it's not because I don't love you. A part of me will always love you. We shared so many memories together. We saw so many sights together. We had so many good times. When we went on dates, to restaurants, to pubs, to clubs, to the beach, swimming, all those exotic holidays.

"And then we'd go home and curl up in bed, and you would have your arms around me, telling me how much you loved me, telling me how much I meant to you. Kissing my forehead, giving me reassurance, telling me that you wanted to spend the rest of your life with me. And our future… It was robbed from us. Time was cut so short for us.

"You were a good man, baby. And God will appreciate that. He'll forgive you for anything wrong that you've done, and you'll be in a better place right now. You're better off in heaven than living in this cruel, fucked-up world. You were a hard-working man, so charming, so sweet, so charismatic. You were gorgeous, with your tanned skin, your black hair, your rugged beard, your chiselled, defined body. And it's not your fault that you were killed by thugs, by scum that don't deserve to be here. I miss you. I miss you so much. I miss your laugh, all the conversations we had. I miss everything.

"But I know that it's time for me to move on. I can't dwell on the past forever. It's been years now. Years of me being heartbroken, miserable, depressed. Unable to even bring myself to look at another man, unable to even bring myself to socialise with other people without feeling like I was going to break down into tears. I've dedicated my life to seeking vengeance for you... But I know now that that's no longer an option. I can't keep pursuing dead trails.

"I hope you know that I did my best. And I hope that you don't hate me for saying all this. Because as much as I loved you, Alejandro, I need to learn to love again. I want to learn to be happy again. I'm tired of being so miserable all the time, I'm tired of dwelling on what I can't change. I know that this is the first stage of acceptance. Accepting that it doesn't matter what I do, what I say... It's not going to bring you back. It's not going to bring you back to me."

I could feel myself quivering, my body trembling and convulsing into a frenzy, as I felt all of my emotions pour out of me, my raw heart out on the surface. I shakily pressed my lips against Alejandro's tombstone, knowing that it was the end.

"I'll always love you, Alejandro. I loved you ever since I first laid eyes on you. Ever since we met, ever since you made me your girlfriend, and then later proposed to me and made me your wife. But if you love me as much as I love you... I need you to free me. I need you to set me free from the chains and shackles of my life. So this will be the last time you see me. I needed closure...

"Goodbye, Alejandro. Gone... But never forgotten. And I hope that when God decides that it's my time too, that it's my turn to die... That I see you again one day in the afterlife. I love you."

And with that, I shakily got to my feet, trembling, and began making my way out of the graveyard.

No turning back…

Not wanting to turn back.

It felt like a massive weight had been lifted off of my shoulders.

A massive burden gone.

I'd got the closure I'd so desperately needed.

I'd said all of the things I needed to say.

And it was now, that I knew…

I knew I would be alright without him.

Because I'd finally accepted things for how they were, and learnt that pain and constantly emotionally torturing myself wasn't the solution to moving forward.

TWO YEARS
LATER

5
ROSE

It had been two whole years now, ever since I'd been to the cemetery to speak to Alejandro, and got the closure I needed.

I felt a lot better. I'd learnt to move on from him, and eventually, I learnt to fall out of love with him, too.

Knowing that it was the best way forward for me.

I decided to begin taking control over my own life, and for the sake of my sanity, adjust to having a normal lifestyle again.

Ever since Alejandro had died, I'd been a hermit for many years. I couldn't even look at another man, yet alone socialise with anybody else without feeling like I was going to break down in tears.

But ever since I'd got the closure I needed, I decided to stop with my isolated stage.

I began to focus on work, to put my all into my accounting career. To work as many hours as I could, and make as much money as possible, to make a good living for myself.

Devoting myself to work enabled me to remain distracted, stay focused, and stay so busy to the point that I would forget about my own feelings.

Not only that, I decided to go out more too. To go out with friends, whether they were from work, or my old university and college friends.

We went to lots of nice places and hung out together, from restaurants, to theme parks, to takeaways, to ice-skating.

And human interaction was something that I didn't realise I'd missed so much.

Something I didn't realise how much I needed.

How much I'd missed.

I didn't have a mother and father around. They passed away when I was young, and I consequently lived alone, so friends were my best bet for now.

I hadn't met another man yet to move on from Alejandro with. But I had had a few one-night stands. Just sex, nothing more.

Friends with benefits, where we had a mutual arrangement that there would be no strings attached. In all honesty, I didn't think I was ready for a serious relationship for a short while, because of how mentally exhausted and drained I was from my last one.

It felt good to have sex though, since I hadn't had it for so many years. Hadn't felt the touch of a man for so many years.

But in all honesty, now that it had been two years on from my closure…

I felt ready.

Ready to have a relationship with another man.

To put my energy and time into another man.

To be loved by another man…

And to love him.

Because I deserved to be happy.

Especially after everything I'd been through…

I deserved it.

I wanted to be loved, to feel loved.

To feel an emotional connection with another man now that I'd moved on from Alejandro.

To have a family of my own…

For a man to want and appreciate me, with all of my flaws, all of my imperfections.

Want me for me.

I just hoped that God would put the right man in my pathway soon…

Because until I met the right man, I would have to keep on having friends with benefits for now.

It didn't fill the void…

But it sure as heck felt good.

6
ACE

I stared out of my balcony, the place I always came to think about life when shit got too heavy.

Taking a cigarette into my mouth and lighting the end of it, I began taking deep puffs of it in and out.

My chest heaving upwards and downwards, rising up and down with each inhalation.

I thought about business, about money, all of the stress on my shoulders.

All of the expectations I always had on me for shit to go right.

I stared out at the beautiful city centre skyline view of Barcelona, the vibrant life, the people, the buildings, the cars, the bright lights.

My home...

My phone was blaring in my pocket, but I didn't care.

For just one night...

I wanted to forget about business.

To forget about my responsibilities.

Suddenly, I heard the pacing of footsteps behind me.

I turned around to come face-to-face with my brother Leonardo.

He took after me, with tanned skin, black hair tied up in a manbun, a stubbly beard, pale green eyes and thick black eyebrows.

We were similar in appearance.

"Hey Ace," Leonardo shrugged, as he joined my side.

"What's up, Leonardo?" I asked.

"I came to let you know that the money from the offshore bank accounts transferred successfully into the casino," Leonardo stated matter-of-factory, folding his arms. "So we're all done for tonight. Bellick said you weren't picking up your calls."

"Yeah... I had some shit on my mind," I muttered. "Good to know it all went smoothly though, without any heat from the feds. That's one less fucking thing for me to stress about."

"Well you're alright to relax now, Bellick and the other guys are taking care of all the other shit we have that needs doing. Collecting the remaining debts we have round the area."

"Good."

I let out a sigh that I didn't know I was holding, before staring back out of my balcony.

"Hey, are you alright, bro?" Leonardo asked, concerned. "Is something bothering you?"

"Yeah," I gritted through clenched teeth. "One word. Maricruz."

Leonardo rolled his eyes.

"Why are you still hung up about that, bro? It's not the end of the world, Jesus fucking Christ. Stop wallowing in self-pity like a little sorry ass bitch."

"That's easy for you to say, you're not the one who has to fucking marry her," I snarled.

"I don't see the fucking problem. She's pretty, she's got a nice body. It's not like *Padre* set you up with an ugly bitch."

"That's besides the fucking point and you know it, Leonardo. Get off my fucking back," I sneered.

"Getting married isn't the be all and fucking end all. It's just a piece of paper. You can still do the same shit you're doing right now, fucking broads, focusing on business. But you know that you have to marry her, whether you like it or fucking not. You have to step up for the family. It's your responsibility."

"I'm fucking done with responsibilities," I gritted, rolling my eyes, balling my hands into fists and rattling them angrily.

"Stop speaking like this, Ace. You're pissing me off. What the fuck's gotten into you?"

Leonardo trailed off his sentence, seething.

"It's our obligation to serve the Corsican Mafia, it's the life we were fucking born into, the life we were born to lead. It's not fair for you to say all this shit, defying Padre's wishes. He's getting old and frail, the least you can do is listen to what he fucking tells you to do in his last years."

"If Padre half cared about us as much as we cared about him, he wouldn't be forcing me to marry this bitch Maricruz in the first place."

I ran my hands through my hair stressfully, sweating profusely as the wind lapped in my face.

Just wishing that things could be different.

"Well instead of working yourself up into a state and stressing yourself out about this, why don't you take some time to cool off instead of pissing yourself off about something you can't fucking change?"

Leonardo raised an eyebrow at me.

I folded my arms bitterly.

"Do you want me to come and take you out for a drink? Let's celebrate the casino's money injection at least," Leonardo shrugged.

"You know I love you, bro. I just haven't been feeling right lately," I sighed.

"Yeah... I know. So how about it then?"

"I appreciate the offer, Leonardo," I heaved. "But tonight, I wanna be on my own. I'll go out for a drink... But without you. Without anybody else."

"Fair enough, bro," Leonardo replied, nodding. "Call me if you need anything."

He took steps closer to me, closing the gap between us.

"Just know what a big favour you're doing the family by marrying Maricruz. Her pops, her family... We need them as alliances. It's good for business. You know that, I know that... and Padre knows that too."

"Yeah," I muttered, and without another word, I turned on my heel and made my way out of the penthouse, slamming the door shut behind me.

7
ACE

I slid into my Mercedes and began driving to the nearest bar, the Casa Lucio. I allowed the wind to lap in my face as I drove faster and faster, picking up speed with each passing second.

Thirty miles per hour...

Forty miles per hour...

Fifty miles per hour…

It wasn't long before I arrived. I pulled the car up to the curb and made my way inside, ready to get hammered.

Needing to forget about all of my problems…

Even if it was just for tonight.

8
ROSE

I sat in bed watching Peaky Blinders on the television. I was on the third season. It was a show about a man called Tommy Shelby and his gangster family, following the life they led in Birmingham, a city in the United Kingdom.

It was a Friday night. I glanced at the clock, and saw that the time had just passed eight P.M.

As much as I was enjoying watching Peaky Blinders, I really couldn't bear the thought of being alone in my apartment on a Friday night munching on cookies, when everyone else in the world was probably out clubbing or getting laid.

I laughed to myself, before taking my phone from my bedside table, ready to call my friend Mezoria from work.

"Hey Mezoria?" I said down the line. "Do you have any plans tonight?"

"No, my boyfriend cancelled on me to go out with his boys," Mezoria retorted huffily. "What are you doing tonight?"

"I'm just watching Peaky Blinders," I replied.

"I love that show. Do you want me to come round and we can watch it together?"

"Why don't we go out?" I asked. "We haven't been out for a while. We could go bowling, or to the arcade or something."

'Sure hun, I'd love to. But not bowling. Something else."

"What do you have in mind?" I asked.

"I want to go to the bar," she declared.

"Are you sure that's the best idea, with your terrible tolerance to alcohol?" I giggled.

"I want to wear something sexy and take snaps for my boyfriend, so he wishes that he stayed inside with me," she giggled in response. "It'll be fun watching him get worked up while he's with his boys but I'm in the bar."

I couldn't help but to break out into a fit of laughter.

"You're so evil."

"Tell me about it."

"Alright, let's go to the bar. Get ready and I'll meet you in town. We can take a cab from there."

"You got it, girl. I'll be ready in about half an hour."

"I'll see you then!" I exclaimed, and hung up the phone.

And then I began walking over to my wardrobe, ready to scorch through all of my outfits.

If Mezoria was going to dress sexy tonight…

Then it was only right that I did, too.

9
ROSE

I settled on wearing a tight red minidress which emphasised my large double G cup bust, my small waist and my thick thighs. I was a plus size woman, so I didn't have a flat belly, but I loved the way that I was shaped.

I knew that being thick wasn't every man's type, but I didn't care. Over time, I'd learnt to love myself the way I was, and I wouldn't change it for the world.

It didn't matter that I didn't look like viral Instagram models or somebody from a Fashion Nova magazine, who had perky tits, huge asses, slim thighs, tiny waists and the flattest stomachs. Everybody was pretty in their own way.

I left my apartment and made my way down to town, ready to meet Mezoria, switching off the television and slamming the door shut behind me.

When I arrived at town, Mezoria was already there, looking pretty with her defined, pale face, her bright red lips, wearing a tight navy midi dress which enunciated her pear-shaped body.

"Hey Mezoria, you look so pretty!" I exclaimed.

"So do you, girl!"

"Looking like that... Let's just say your boyfriend will be getting rattled for sure seeing the pictures you send him."

She giggled in response.

"Let's go, babe. It's getting cold standing outside."

"Yeah. Let me call a cab."

We waited patiently for the cab, and soon later, we set off for the bar.

The Casa Lucio.

10
ACE

"Vodka tonic please," I sighed to the barman, as I slumped down into my seat.

"Rough day, huh?"

"Something like that," I muttered.

"Coming right up."

I waited patiently for him to pour me my drink, and as soon as he handed it over to me, I wasted no time in swallowing it down in one gulp, allowing it to burn down my throat.

I let out a satisfied sigh.

"Another one please."

"Coming right up."

He poured me another…

And I drank it.

Then it was another, and another, and another.

But my alcohol tolerance was so high…

I couldn't even get drunk.

I could feel my phone begin to blare and vibrate into a frenzy in the pocket of my black jacket.

I took it out, and looked at the name that was blaring across the screen.

Maricruz.

She was definitely going to get fucking ignored.

I rolled my eyes again. Just as I was about to ask the barman for another drink, I could see something from the corner of my eye.

Something that had sparked my curiosity.

I found myself turning away from the barman, narrowing my eyes, wanting to focus on who I'd just saw.

And what I found myself laying eyes on…

Was the most beautiful woman I'd ever seen in my entire life.

11
ACE

I cocked my head to the side, as I drunk her in.

Her beautiful, sexy fucking face, her delicious body that was made for sin.

She was built and shaped like a goddess.

Meaty, with the most beautiful tits I'd seen.

Just how I liked my women.

Long hair, big, plump pouty lips covered in lipgloss that would look good wrapped around my fucking cock.

Arched eyebrows, thick thighs, hip dips, a nice belly.

I loved meat on my women...

And she looked good enough to fucking eat.

She was everything that Maricruz wasn't.

Sure, Maricruz was pretty...

But she wasn't even my type.

Maricruz was slim, the complete opposite of the woman who I was laying eyes on right now.

Hell, why couldn't Padre get me an arranged marriage to a woman like this?

12

ACE

I stared at her intently, just appreciating and taking in how beautiful she really was.

She was standing with her friend, and almost every man in the bar had their eyes on her right now.

Hell, if I didn't want to punch their fucking faces and shoot down all of these bastards for even thinking they had a chance with her.

I saw her first.

I'd already staked my fucking claim.

If these men thought that they could try and take what was mine…

Then they had another thing fucking coming.

She made her way to the bar with her friend, calling for the barman to buy a drink.

But as soon as she did, her eyes met with mine as she noticed me from across the room.

Her cheeks began to flush bright pink as she began smiling nervously, a dimple forming in her fucking cheek.

Jesus fucking Christ.

She turned to her friend, as if she was trying to distract herself by speaking to her, but I never once stopped looking at her.

She glanced at me again, her face still burning, tucking her hair behind her ear, looking up at me with those big brown fuck-me eyes.

As if she was starting to get insecure underneath my gaze.

Hell, she had nothing to be insecure about.

She didn't know just how sexy I found her.

And I would show her just how sexy I found her in due time, too.

13
ROSE

When me and Mezoria arrived at the bar, and I was about to call the barman for our drinks, I saw somebody from the corner of my eye sitting on the other side of the bar.

And he was staring right at me.

Intently…

As if he'd been watching me for a long time.

When our eyes met, I couldn't help but to feel my skin burn underneath his gaze, feeling myself getting flustered just at the sight of him.

He was easily the sexiest man I'd ever laid eyes on.

With thick eyebrows, tanned skin, a scruffy beard, beautiful black hair.

And then there was his *body*.

He was wearing a tight black jacket, leaving little to the imagination about how well-built his frame was.

I could feel my breath catch in my throat, not sure what he wanted with me.

Not sure if he was staring at me out of curiosity…

Or because he actually wanted to speak to me.

But seeing as he hadn't said a word to me yet…

I thought so much that he didn't want to say anything.

I swallowed down a lump in my throat, before shutting off my thoughts, needing to stop myself from getting distracted by him.

I came here with Mezoria tonight...

And I needed to remember that.

14
ACE

I continued to watch her intently.

I called the barman on my side of my table, and told him to pay for her and her friend's drinks all night.

He nodded obediently.

I could feel my phone begin to vibrate again.

Texts from Maricruz...

But I couldn't be bothered to read them.

I didn't want to think about her and the arrangement tonight.

I continued to watch her and her friend.

Speaking to each other...

Giggling together.

She still exchanged glances with me, but they were short-lived.

A few men tried approaching her, asking her for her number...

But they said no to all of them.

And I could feel the corners of my mouth curling upwards into a satisfied smirk.

Knowing that I was the only man in the room who'd made an impact on her.

It wasn't long before a man approached her friend, exchanging flirtatious gestures, before taking her away from her, to the main floor, where they were dancing together.

Leaving the woman alone.

Now it was *my* turn to talk to her.

15
ACE

I made my way over to her.

"What's your name then, gorgeous?" I asked, closing the space between us, to the point I could hear her erratic breathing and heartbeat.

I'd already had this impact on her just looking at her...

I could only imagine what would happen if things went further.

"My name is none of your concern," she remarked, folding her arms, but she was smiling.

"Playing hard to get, huh?" I smirked. "Because the way you were looking over me back then... Told a completely different story."

Her cheeks burned bright red again, before she coughed loudly.

"It's Rose," she smiled, with her hands on her hips. "And you?"

"Ace," I replied.

She twirled her hair around her finger, biting down on her lip.

God, she was so fucking sexy.

"If you don't mind me saying, you're absolutely gorgeous," I rasped, my pupils dilating, my eyes darkening with desire as I took all of her face and frame in from up close.

She was ten times as fucking beautiful up close.

"Thank you," she blushed, scratching her arm nervously. "You're not so bad yourself."

I let out a low chuckle.

"Oh, I know that, darling. Or you wouldn't be speaking to me right now... You'd be ignoring me just like you ignored all the other motherfuckers in this room tonight."

16
ACE

"I take it you've had quite a bit to drink then?" I asked her, smirking.

"Nope. I wasn't in the mood for it tonight," she replied.

"You know, Rose..." I cocked my head to the side, biting my lip. "I'm gonna be straight to the point. I like you."

Her cheeks started burning again, but she didn't say anything.

"Your friend is clearly occupied, so you're here on your own now. And I am, too."

"She has a boyfriend. She's only dancing with another man to send him videos... Make him furious."

I let out an amused chuckle.

"Cheeky of her."

I narrowed my eyes intently.

"So, what do you say?"

I trailed off my sentence, my eyes locking with hers.

"You wanna get out of here?"

"I'm not gonna fuck you," she remarked huffily. "If that's what you came here for. I don't make it a habit of fucking men I don't know."

"Oh baby, I know," I rasped. "I was going to take you for a drive, get a little change of scene since neither of us want any more drinks. I'm a gentleman. I don't fuck on the first date."

She looked a little embarrassed, as if she was instantly regretting what she'd just said.

"Sorry. I didn't mean to seem rude," she mumbled.

I let out a low, amused chuckle.

"It's cool. You were just being cautious."

"So, a drive huh?" she asked, smiling. "What makes you so confident that I wanna go with you? You could be a serial killer for all I know."

"Well you're just going to have to trust me then, aren't you *mami*?" I remarked, still smirking.

Her defiance, the way she was making me chase her and work for it…

Made me want her that much fucking more.

I took another step closer to her. At this point, I was so close to her, that if I leant forward, we'd end up fucking kissing. I was having a hard time restraining myself with how beautiful she was.

"I know you want me just as much as I want you, mami."

She blushed beetroot red, before swallowing.

"Alright. I'll come with you."

I let out a satisfied chuckle.

This woman didn't have the slightest idea who I really was, what I really dealt with in my line of business.

Her words rung in my head.

You could be a serial killer, for all I know.

I suddenly found myself sweating profusely, knowing that I was no good for her.

Knowing that I was being a selfish fucking bastard just by pursuing her tonight.

But I had to remind myself that tonight was just about forgetting about my real life.

So as much as I was taking a liking to this woman…

I would just have to forget about her once the night was over.

Forget I ever crossed paths with her…

Forget that this night ever happened.

Forget I ever met her.

And then go back home to my Padre, to Leonardo…

And marry Maricruz for the sake of the family.

17
ACE

She took my hand in hers as we left the bar.

"One second… Let me just message my friend Mezoria so that she knows I've left."

"Sure thing," I shrugged.

She quickly tapped into her keypad, before turning her phone off and shoving it back into her pocket.

And on second thoughts…

I turned off my phone, too.

Not wanting anything to get in the way of me enjoying Rose tonight.

18
ACE

We made our way into my Mercedes, and I could see her jaw drop in awe as she looked at the car.

"Wow... It's beautiful," she commented, as she slid into the passenger seat.

She looked so fucking pretty sitting in the passenger seat.

"Thank you," I replied, smiling.

Not fazed by this compliment, since I had about one-hundred other expensive cars sitting at home.

Too many possessions...

More than I knew what to do with.

"What do you do for a living?" she asked.

"I'm a businessman," I said, which wasn't a complete lie, she just didn't know what *kind* of business.

"That's lovely," she replied, smiling. "I'm an accountant."

"Brains and beauty, babe."

She let out a small giggle.

She looked so pretty when she laughed, fuck me. I stared at her dress, her beautiful red bodycon dress that I just wanted to tear off with my teeth.

I needed to distract myself, anything from her body and face, because I kept getting visions of me spreading her legs across the back of my car and eating her pussy like I was a starved fucking man.

I bet she tasted just as sweet as she fucking sounded, just as sweet as she looked.

And I found myself growing more and more frustrated with just the sinful thoughts that were running through my mind right now, my cock rubbing painfully against the cloth of my trousers.

"Are you okay?" she asked, raising an eyebrow.

"Yeah." I coughed loudly. "I was just thinking about something."

Thinking about what it would be like having those delicious tits in my mouth.

She tucked her hair behind her hair nervously.

"So… Where are you taking me then, Ace? What's the destination?"

I let out a low chuckle.

"I know a nice spot. You'll love it, mami."

19
ACE

I drove down to the beach on the other side of town, knowing that women loved that kind of shit.

Scenery, sand, water.

And I would be lying if I didn't say I loved it, too.

The calm, peaceful feeling.

I played slow, soft songs in the background as we drove together, and she began getting more comfortable around me.

"How's a beautiful lady like you single, mami?" I found myself asking her, letting out a low chuckle.

She swallowed down a lump in her throat, as she stared out of the window.

"My husband died many years ago."

I could feel my cheeks burn, suddenly feeling terrible for asking her.

She turned to me, noticing my discomfort.

"It's okay, I'm over him," she shrugged. "I just haven't met anybody that I like enough to pursue a relationship ever since."

My tensed shoulders relaxed. I put my hand on her thigh, giving it a reassuring squeeze.

"Maybe you met him tonight," I said carefully.

You're a fucking bastard, I thought to myself.

You're stringing her along for nothing.

You know that you're leaving her after tonight.

20
ACE

She placed her hand over mine, feeling comforted by my touch. She leaned in closer for a split-second, as if she was about to kiss me, but then her breath caught in her throat. Hesitating, she moved backwards, as if she instantly regretted the move she'd made.

"Why did you move back?" I asked her, as I continued to rotate the steering wheel.

"I -" she stumbled. "I don't know. I hardly know you."

"So what? There's no rules. No boundaries when it comes to seeing someone."

I trailed off my sentence.

"You can get to know me."

Her eyes burned into mine.

"How can something feel so wrong... but so right at the same time?"

"Just relax, babe. Don't overthink things too much. If you want to take it slow... Then I'll respect your wishes. I'm not a dick."

She gave me a small smile.

"Thank you."

I smiled back, as we pulled up the car.

We'd arrived at our destination.

21
ACE

We made our way out of the car, and leant against it as we stared out at the beach from on top of a cliff.

Watching the waves crash onto the shore, watching the night continue to take its course.

"You know, I didn't expect you to be like this," Rose murmured softly.

I let out a low chuckle.

"What do you mean?" I asked her.

"Back at the bar... You looked really intimidating. Dominant. A man who knows what he wants."

She trailed off her sentence, letting out a low giggle.

"But you're a big softie. So gentle, so caring. I really like it."

"I can do both, mami," I growled in a voice I didn't recognise, as I watched her breath catch in her throat.

I inched closer to her, allowing my hand to move upwards to stroke her face.

"Rough. Nasty. Fast. I can do it all."

A moan escaped from her lips as I said this, and it drove me to the brink of insanity.

Knowing it was just my words doing this to her.

Let alone my fucking touch.

"Fuck," she moaned. "That's so sexy."

"Because you're so sexy," I growled. "Fuck taking it slow. I want you. I want all of you, fuck."

"I want you too," she whimpered breathlessly.

That was the only confirmation I needed.

I crashed my mouth down on hers, kissing her with everything I had inside of me.

Knowing that there would be no turning back after this.

I would never be able to forget her.

The sweetest fucking sin.

The beautiful busty brunette, who'd turned my life upside down from the minute she fucking stepped in it.

Rose.

22
ACE

She tangled her hands in my hair, pulling me closer almost desperately.

She never stopped whimpering against my fucking mouth.

She wrapped her thighs tightly around my body as I pushed her harder against the car, to the point that she could feel how hard and hot I was for her.

She slipped her tongue into mine as she kissed me with urgency, causing a guttural moan to escape from my throat.

She was driving me crazy.

She was driving me fucking crazy.

"Oh God, Ace…" she moaned, sliding her tongue into my mouth, her tongue playing with mine in a fury.

Each touch, each lick…

Left me aching for more.

Knowing that I would never be able to get enough of this woman now that I'd tasted her just once.

I allowed my hands to trail down her the arch of her back, leaving her breathless as I ran my fingers up and down at a torturous pace, not able to get enough of hearing her delicious fucking moans.

She was consuming me.

My mind, my body, my soul.

She was mine.

Mine to kiss, mine to touch.

Mine to *torture*.

I'd be damned if I ever let another man have her. It didn't matter if I'd only met her a few hours ago. She'd completely ruined me.

Jesus fucking Christ.

23
ACE

"Ace, please…"

She moaned uncontrollably against my mouth, as I continued to run my fingers up and down her body.

Every delicious curve, from the slim of her waist, to her beautiful, thick, juicy thighs, back up to her voluptuous fucking tits.

I moved the straps of her dress down her shoulders, before taking her breasts into my hands, squeezing them, massaging them, feeling myself groan just at the sheer size of them.

She was so busty…

So fucking *busty*.

I twisted her nipples, never once stopping my tongue from exploring her mouth as she whimpered and quivered against my touch.

"Ace…"

The way she was moaning my name was turning me the fuck on.

To the point that there was no turning back.

Growing more and more frustrated against her, knowing that it would never be enough.

I let out another growl, moving my lips away from her mouth, trailing wet kisses down from her neck to her collarbone.

Licking, biting, sucking, needing to mark my fucking territory.

Needing to ruin her for any other man.

Needing her to forget that she'd ever been touched by another man before...

Because now...

She was *mine*.

She belonged to me.

24
ACE

I tore her lacy bra off with my teeth, before taking her nipples into my mouth, as her eyes rolled backwards and she began to scream.

I allowed my free hand to move under her dress, fingering her wetness, rubbing her clit in a circular motion, at a torturous pace that had her begging for more.

"You're so fucking wet. So fucking sexy," I moaned uncontrollably.

I continued to lap my tongue at her nipple, before plunging my fingers inside of her, needing to feel her rock against them, needing to feel her sweet juices all over my hand.

"Ace, please..." she moaned, throwing her head back in pleasure, roughly knotting her hands in my hair as she pulled my mouth away from her succulent fucking tits back up to her mouth.

I took my fingers out of her before putting them into my mouth, licking every drop. She tasted so fucking good, so fucking sweet, just like I fucking anticipated, and it was pushing me over the fucking brink.

She watched me lick my fingers and never once stopped moaning, before I crashed my mouth back down on hers, needing her to taste herself from my lips.

It was so erotic...

So fucking sexy.

My hands moved down to her ass, allowing myself to play with it.

Her ass was so fat, round, bouncy and jiggly, it was causing my vision to fog.

I was immersed in her.

Intoxicated by her.

Intoxicated by her…

Intoxicated by her touch.

I picked her up, readying myself for her, allowing her to grip onto me for more support.

She moved her hand to my crotch, rubbing up and down it, as I grew harder and harder against her.

All of the self-restraint, all of the control that I had in my body…

Was long gone.

Long fucking gone.

I was so ready.

So ready to take her…

To plunge myself inside of her, to rock her world, knowing that she would pleasure herself thinking back to this night, knowing that she was all fucking mine.

But before I could take it any further…

I heard a loud crashing sound behind me, and it caused me to snap straight out of my trance.

Completely extinguishing the bubble I had shared tonight with Rose…

As reality hit me back in the face from a million different directions at once.

25
ACE

I turned around abruptly, finding myself jolt upwards in shock.

Rose quivered into a frenzy beside me, horror-stricken, a terrified expression etched all over her face.

I'd ruined her.

I'd ruined her fucking innocence…

Because now…

She was seeing something that she would *never* be able to forget.

Never be able to shake from her damn mind.

"A – Ace…" she quivered. "W – What's going on?"

A black, glossy AMG pulled up to the area.

And I knew that something terrible was going to happen, from the minute I turned around and laid eyes on it…

Because I *recognised* that car.

It had tinted windows, and suddenly, the doors opened wide.

Leonardo clambered outside of it.

And he wasn't alone.

26
ACE

Leonardo was dragging out a man from the car.

A man that I didn't recognise.

And he was holding a gun against his temple.

"Leonardo," I swallowed. "What's going on?"

"You don't know how to answer your phone?" Leonardo snarled, slamming the man down onto the floor, so that he fell against it with a hard and painful smack. "I had to fucking track your car to fucking find you and get a hold of you."

Rose let out a blood-curdling scream beside me, as she began sobbing.

"It was switched off," I gritted through clenched teeth. "I'm not entitled to any privacy now, am I not? You were the one who told me to forget about business for tonight, to go out and enjoy myself. Backfired on me now, huh?"

I could feel my veins pulsate, making their way onto the surface of my skin alarmingly, suddenly seething. So much rage roaring through my body in this moment, that it felt like my blood was boiling to the point it almost dried up.

I was with a woman.

An innocent woman…

And Leonardo had brought our personal business here.

So much for forgetting things just for one night.

"You're to keep your phone on at all times. You know the fucking rules, Ace!" Leonardo roared. "Check your phone. CHECK YOUR PHONE RIGHT NOW!"

I swallowed down a lump in my throat, before giving him a small nod.

I took my phone out of my pocket, switching it on.

Knowing that I wasn't ready for what I was about to see.

27
ACE

"Maricruz left you about a hundred messages, you fucking bastard. Didn't even have the decency to reply to your fucking soon-to-be wife?"

"S – soon to be wife?" Rose whispered, her voice hollow and empty.

Fuck.

I hadn't wanted her to find out about all of this shit like this…

I swallowed, opening my text messages, and read the messages from Maricruz.

Ace, where are you?!

It's urgent.

I need your help!

A man has broken into the house, I'm all alone at home, I can hear so much shooting!

Please come!

He's shooting down the guards!

I'm all alone, Ace, please…

I'm really scared!

He's shooting down all the guards, what if he does something to me?!

I could feel my heart thump against my chest into a frenzy, as I began sweating profusely, suddenly feeling like complete and utter shit in this moment.

I felt so terrible…

So damn fucking terrible.

It felt like the walls were closing in on me.

Like I was suffocating…

And I couldn't breathe.

I couldn't fucking breathe.

"I – is she okay?" I swallowed.

"No. We couldn't get there in time to save her," Leonardo snarled.

"W – what?" I croaked. "What the fuck happened?!"

"She was shot down by a man from a rival cartel. Left for dead. Bled out… By the time the doctors got to her, she was already gone."

"FUCK!" I roared. "Fuck… This wasn't supposed to happen…"

I hadn't wanted to marry Maricruz…

But I wished no ill upon her.

I sure as hell didn't want her fucking dead.

It felt like my heart was being ripped out of my chest in this very fucking moment, the guilt almost consuming me entirely.

She'd messaged me countlessly, begging me for help…

And I'd been so busy immersing myself in Rose back at the bar, that I hadn't even bothered to check my messages.

Fuck.

28
ACE

"I see you were too busy getting your dick rode, getting your dusty old trumpet fucking blown, to even bother taking care of the situation," Leonardo seethed, shooting Rose a look of venom, as she continued to sob beside me.

This wasn't her fault…

She couldn't be blamed for the stupid mistake i'd fucking made on my own.

"So what now?" I swallowed.

I took my chain of Christ from around my neck and brought it up to my lips, marking the trinity, just wishing that God would forgive me for my fucking sins.

"Padre is fucking furious, and Maricruz's mother and father are heartbroken. Heartbroken at the fact that in the morning their daughter was alive... And by the evening, she was gone. I bet they'll keep beating themselves up about this for as long as they fucking live."

"I'm so sorry, man. I'm so fucking sorry."

I hung my head.

"I didn't mean for it to come to this. I'm sorry."

Leonardo let out a frustrated sigh, before shaking his head.

"I know you didn't, bro. We've just gotta push forward and take care of the situation. Bring her to justice... Help her parents through this."

"You're right," I replied, wiping the sweat from my forehead.

Needing to get my head back in the game.

"And it starts with this motherfucker right here," Leonardo gritted, kicking the limp body of the man on the ground, as he let out a blood-curdling scream, terror etched all over his face, begging and pleading with us to spare his fucking life. "This is the motherfucker responsible for shooting Maricruz."

29
ACE

I could feel heat roar through my body, and pound through my face, as I became fixated on vengeance.

Fixated on bringing Maricruz to justice.

Bringing her family to justice...

Our strongest alliances.

The Corsican Mafia.

Leonardo bent down next to the bastard's body, freeing him from the rope.

Then he got up, standing on his balls, severing them, causing the man to scream in pain as his face went blue.

"You'll pay for what you did, motherfucker," Leonardo gritted.

"P – please, spare me!" the motherfucker bawled. "I had orders! I didn't want to fucking do it! I didn't have a choice!"

"There's always a choice," I snarled. "You made that choice leading the fucked-up life you live."

I bent down next to his body, and wrapped my hands around his neck, squeezing it, causing him to splutter and choke as he weakened underneath my harsh grasp.

The wind knocking out of his lungs, as he continued to suffocate against my grip.

"WHO SENT YOU?!" I roared.

"The Ndrangheta," he spluttered, as I let out a growl, freeing him from my hands.

"Motherfucker," I snarled, and began punching his face, mercilessly, relentlessly, until I heard his jaw snap, until his teeth began knocking clean out of his mouth, until it was nothing but blood gushing out of his mouth as his face went green and raw with flesh.

30
ACE

"Finish the fucking job," I snarled to Leonardo.

Leonardo nodded, taking his gun out of his pocket, and then shooting the motherfucker three times clean in the chest.

"Good thing we're right next to the sea, so we can dispose of the body fucking easily," Leonardo snarled.

He grabbed hold of the body from one side while I grabbed hold from the other side.

Together, we made our way to the edge of the cliff, tossing the motherfucker out of it, allowing him to drown in the tides.

"Fuck," Leonardo breathed, dusting himself off.

"So, what now?" I asked him.

"You'll need to ring Padre. He's hitting the roof about what happened. Especially when he was so desperate for you to marry Maricruz."

"Yeah, I understand."

I sighed heavily, running my hands through my hair stressfully.

This wasn't how I was expecting tonight to go down at all.

31
ACE

"We have another fucking problem," Leonardo gritted, as I took my phone out, ready to call Padre.

Before I dialled Padre's number into the keypad, I looked up, and saw that Leonardo was nodding straight towards Rose.

I could feel my heart leap to my throat as I turned around to face her.

She was no longer screaming…

She was no longer sobbing.

She'd gone white in shock, as she'd watched the whole situation play itself out in front of her.

She was just an accountant…

An innocent fucking woman.

And now, she'd just witnessed a murder.

The shit a normal girl like her usually only saw in TV shows.

But this was the life I lived on a daily fucking basis.

"Rose," I swallowed, feeling a lump catch in my throat.

I was about to open my mouth to tell her how sorry I was, but then I shook my head, knowing better not to make it even worse.

Saying sorry wouldn't erase everything that had fucking happened.

The words she said back in the bar rung in my head.

You could be a serial killer for all I know.

My heart thumped erratically against my chest, feeling so ashamed of myself in this moment for allowing a girl like her to get involved with a fucked-up monster like me.

The devil him fucking self.

But I knew that the worst was yet to come.

Because the words that Leonardo said next...

Caused the full reality of the situation to hit me from a million different directions at once.

32
ACE

"She's a witness, Ace," Leonardo stated matter-of-factly, folding his arms. "Whatever you two had going on tonight... You know the rules. No witnesses. We have to fucking take care of witnesses."

I heaved my chest, feeling at loss.

Feeling so empty in this fucking moment.

She began quivering again beside me, as if she was preparing herself for what was about to come.

Preparing herself, as if she thought that we were about to fucking kill her.

She wouldn't say a whole word the entire time…

I felt so terrible…

So fucking terrible.

A sudden sound of ringing from my phone caused me to snap out of my thoughts.

"It's Padre," I murmured, as I brought my phone up to my face to read who it was.

I pressed the green 'Receive' button, before holding my phone against my ear.

Ready to listen to what Padre was about to tell me.

33
ACE

"This is a fucking shit show, Ace!" Padre roared down the line. "*¡Se suponía que esto no iba a pasar!*"

This wasn't supposed to fucking happen!

"I know, Padre. I'm sorry."

"You were supposed to marry Maricruz this time next week!" Padre roared.

"*¡Todo se ha ido a la mierda!*"

Everything has gone to shit!

"*¡Todos los planes para la familia se arruinaron!*"

All of the plans for the family ruined!

I swallowed down a lump in my throat, feeling terrible.

Terrible that I'd failed my father.

Terrible that I'd failed my family.

"How can I fix this, Padre?" I asked, my voice hollow.

Knowing that my father was getting frail and weak, just like Leonardo had warned me earlier…

So I wanted to make him happy while I still could.

Knowing that I would regret not doing all I could for him after he was gone.

"You must find somebody else to marry as soon as possible!" Padre gritted. "The wedding is still to go ahead as planned. For the sake of our reputation... Everything needs to go smoothly."

He trailed off his sentence.

"Even if Maricruz will no longer be your bride."

34
ACE

I dialled off my phone, gulping, before shoving it back into my pocket.

Leonardo stared at me with a deathly expression on his face.

"Guess you finally got what you wanted, huh?" He snarled. "Finally free from a marriage with Maricruz."

He cocked his head to the side venomously.

"I bet half of you is glad that this fucking happened."

"Shut the fuck up, Leonardo. Don't fucking piss me off."

I gritted my teeth, flashing him a warning look that made him know I meant business.

Even if he was my brother…

I fucking hated it when people got on my bad side.

When people kept adding more fuel to the fucking fire.

Pissing me off to the point I wanted to suffocate them, strangle them, making them plead for air.

35
ROSE

I continued to watch Ace and his brother bicker with each other.

I could hardly keep myself upright, my eyes fogging with tears, as I recounted everything that had just happened.

I was in a state of confusion, in a state of fucking shock.

Hardly able to come to terms with what happened, or even comprehend it.

I could barely breathe.

It felt like my heart was being ripped out of my chest...

Like somebody was stabbing a million daggers straight through my chest, and twisting them.

This was the second time I'd witnessed a murder.

The first time being with Alejandro...

The second time being right now.

And it brought all the bad memories I'd tried so hard to shut away...

Straight back to the surface.

The way they tossed the body into the river, as if they were unfazed by what they were doing, like human life was worthless, and so easily disposable...

It made me sick to my stomach.

I hadn't expected this from Ace.

I knew that he was a complete stranger.

I knew that I'd trusted him too easily tonight.

Allowing myself to leave the bar alone, with a man that I didn't even know.

Allowing myself to get intimate with him.

To share a connection with him that I'd never shared with anybody else.

Getting hot and heavy with him, being touched in no way I'd ever been touched before.

Breaking down my walls for him…

Breaking down my boundaries for him.

I'd been so hopeful that tonight was going to go right…

Especially because he kept saying the right things.

Had me hanging off of his every word.

But despite everything I never, *never* in a million years expected this to happen.

And now…

I knew that I was about to die for being a witness to this whole thing.

The worst was yet to come…

I just hoped that God would forgive me for my sins.

Maybe I would me meeting Alejandro again in heaven sooner than I thought…

36
ACE

"Fuck this argument," I gritted through clenched teeth. "I've got better things to do than go round in fucking circles with you, Leonardo. Cut me some fucking slack."

"Yeah, you do have better things to do," Leonardo snarled. "Like taking care of this whore you've got standing beside you right now."

"Don't call her that," I spewed viciously.

"In case you're forgetting, she's a witness. We need to get rid of her, and then go home to Padre," Leonardo spat bitterly.

37
ACE

I turned to face Rose, just wishing that she knew how sorry I was.

Tonight, she'd rocked my world in a different way.

Left me completely exposed to her.

And the way that she submitted to me…

The way she was completely at my mercy.

Allowing me to do what I pleased with her body.

It screwed with my mind to the point of no fucking return.

I hated the way that shit played out tonight.

Hell, she probably hated me now.

I'd be surprised if she fucking didn't.

I knew that there was only one way to deal with witnesses…

And that was by killing them.

It was the rules of the fucking Mafia.

But as I stared at her, took all of her in, and recounted everything that had happened between us tonight…

I knew that I wouldn't be able to bring myself to fucking do it.

I didn't have the bottle.

I was a pussy.

A sorry-ass bitch, who couldn't finish the war he fucking started.

She stared at me with pleading eyes. She didn't need to say a word, but I knew that she was just begging me to spare her.

I only had myself to fucking blame.

I wanted her for myself.

I wanted to keep her.

To enjoy her for the rest of my fucking life.

I didn't want her to fucking die.

38
ACE

Leonardo cocked the gun in his hands, and passed it over to me.

"Shoot her," he ordered. "Finish what you fucking started."

I shakily took the gun from his hands, bringing it upwards, convulsing as I held the trigger, holding it out in front of Rose.

She was completely frozen to the spot…

Watching her entire life flash before her eyes.

I couldn't do it.

I couldn't fucking do it…

I needed to think of something.

A solution to get her out of this…

And fast.

Without breaking the rules of the mafia.

Sweating profusely, my thoughts scrambled themselves together in my head.

Doing my best to think rationally.

Doing my best to fit the puzzle pieces together in my head.

And then…

Something clicked inside of me.

I remembered the phone call conversation I just had with Padre a few moments ago.

Stating that the marriage needed to go ahead as planned, regardless of Maricruz being out of the picture...

And I found my shoulders tensing, knowing that this solution would be the only way to keep Rose alive.

Knowing that she was going to fucking hate me for it.

But she would have to go ahead with it...

Whether she liked it or not.

No choice in the fucking matter.

I ran my hands through my hair stressfully, before letting out an exasperated growl, tossing the gun to the side, gritting my teeth.

Rose stared at me with a look that was both a mixture of confusion and shock on her face.

She'd come so close to death...

So fucking close.

She had her eyes shut, saying prayers to God the entire time.

And now she had them open…

Wondering why I hadn't pulled the fucking trigger.

"Well?" Leonardo snarled. "You're really gonna pussy out of this, huh?"

I turned around to face him.

"Padre wants me to get married, to find a replacement for Maricruz."

I trailed off my sentence, turning back around to face her, my eyes burning into hers as she quivered, burning underneath my gaze.

"I'm not going to kill this woman."

I stared at her dead in the face.

"I'm going to make her my wife."

And I meant every.

Single.

Word.

TO BE CONTINUED

FIND OUT WHAT HAPPENS NEXT IN CAGED PRINCESS

For updates, follow the author on Instagram @agkbooks

author's note

If you are enjoying this series, then it would mean the world to me if you could leave me a review on, to help other readers to discover my books too, and share it with your friends and family. If you do leave a review, don't hesitate to get in touch with me, and I will thank you personally.